Flower Patterns
coloring book
Volume 1

Illustrated by
Pamela Duarte

I0505137

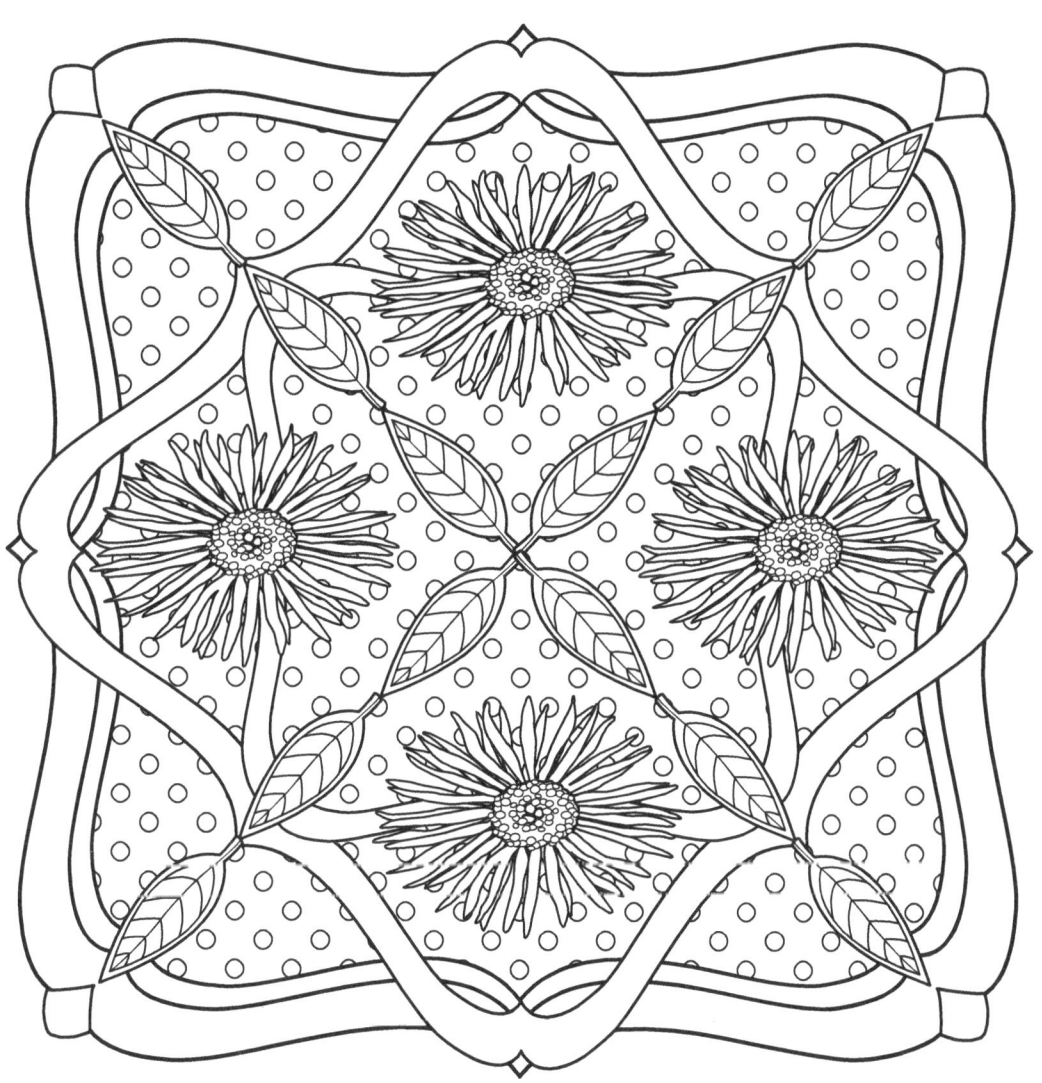

Flower Patterns Coloring Book, Volume 1
©2015 Pamela Duarte

All rights reserved. No part of this book may be reproduced or transmitted by any form or by any means, electronic or mechanical, including photocopy, recording, or any information storage or retrieval system, without prior written consent from the author.

I hope you have as much fun coloring these as I did creating them. Enjoy!

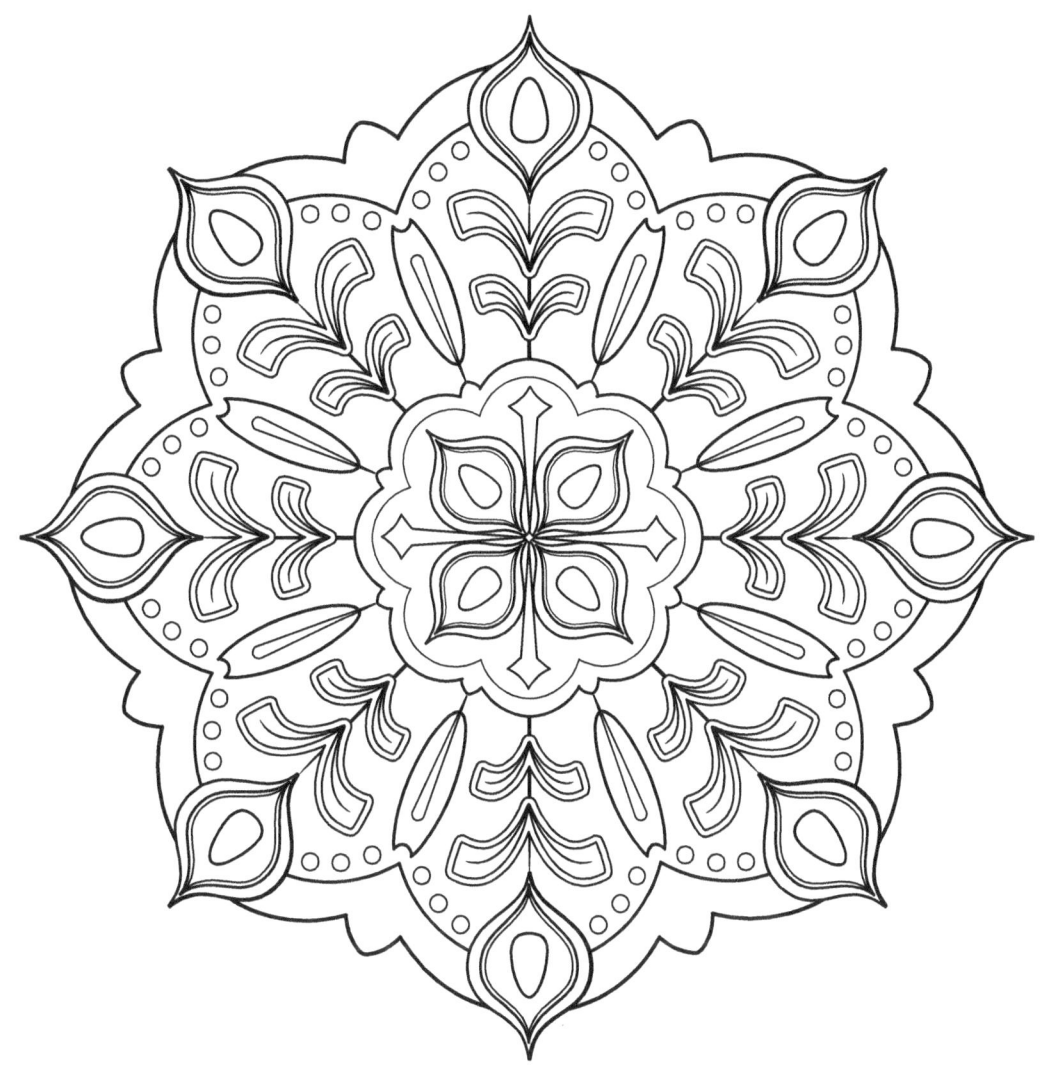

This book is dedicated to:

My beloved Brother, smart, funny, and my closest confidant
and to
Richard Ellescas, my teacher, my mentor,
and most importantly, my friend.

The pages of this book are suitable for colored pencils, markers, and a variety of other media. They are only printed on one side and to help prevent bleed through, please place a blank sheet of paper between the pages when coloring.

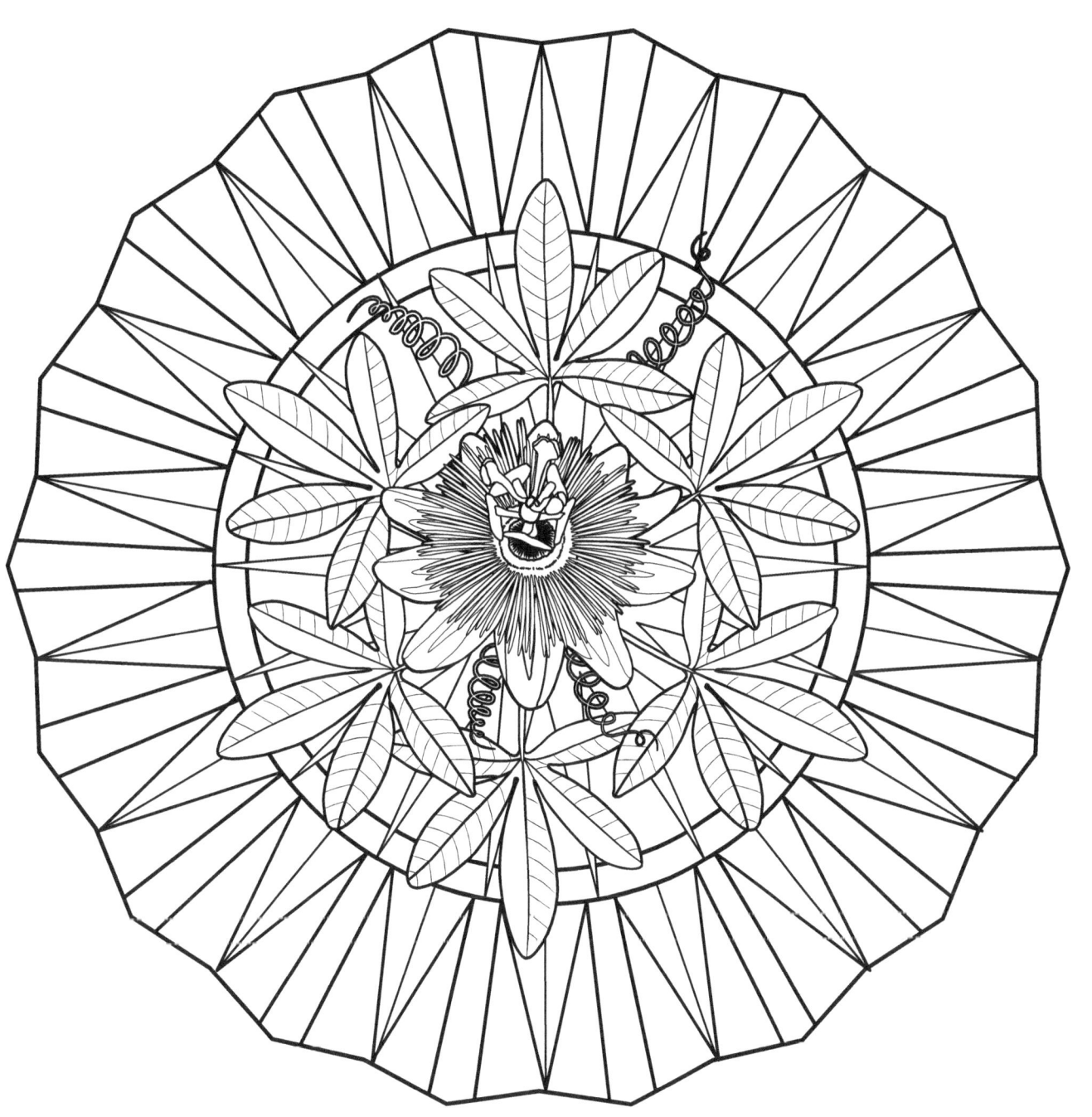

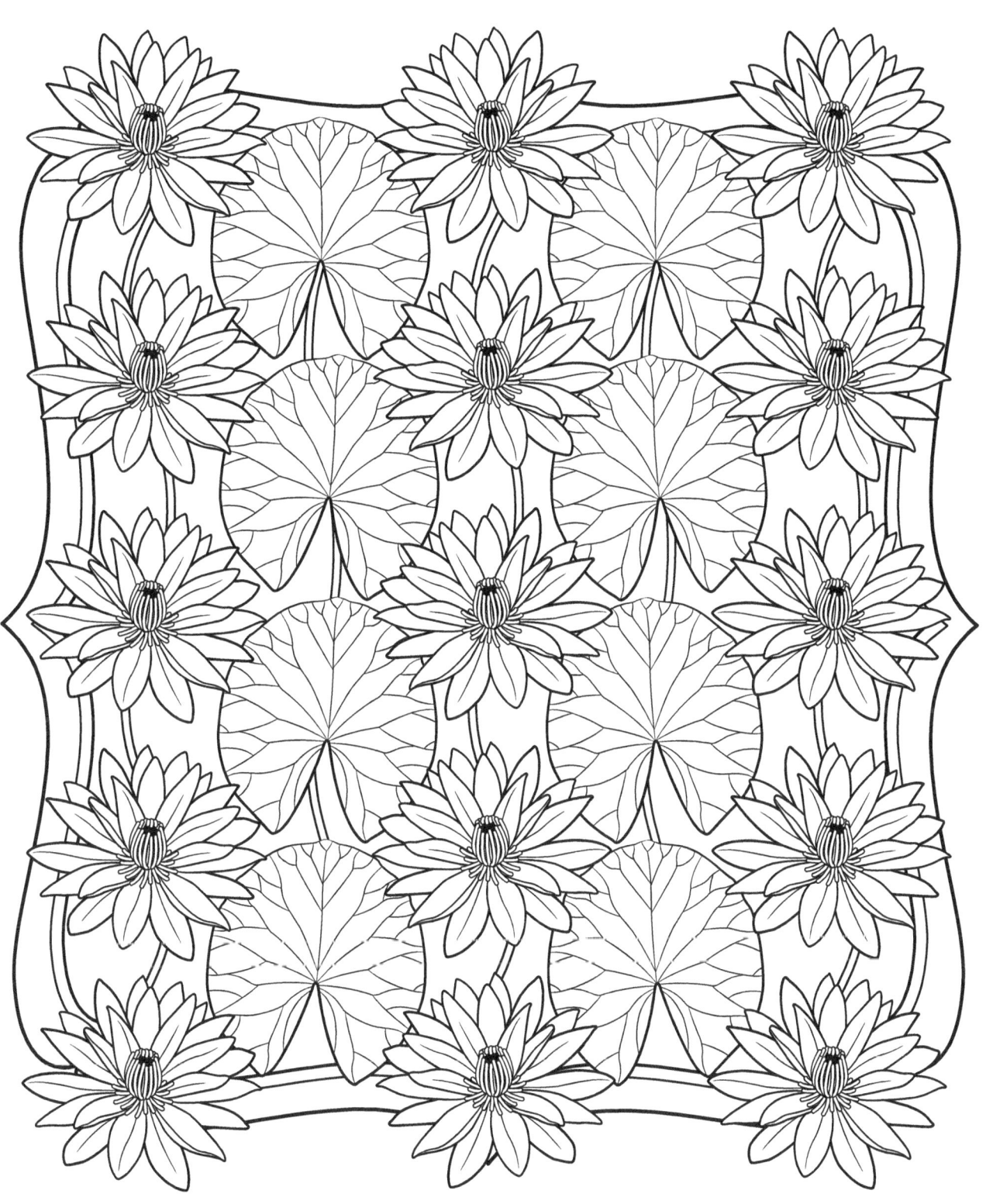

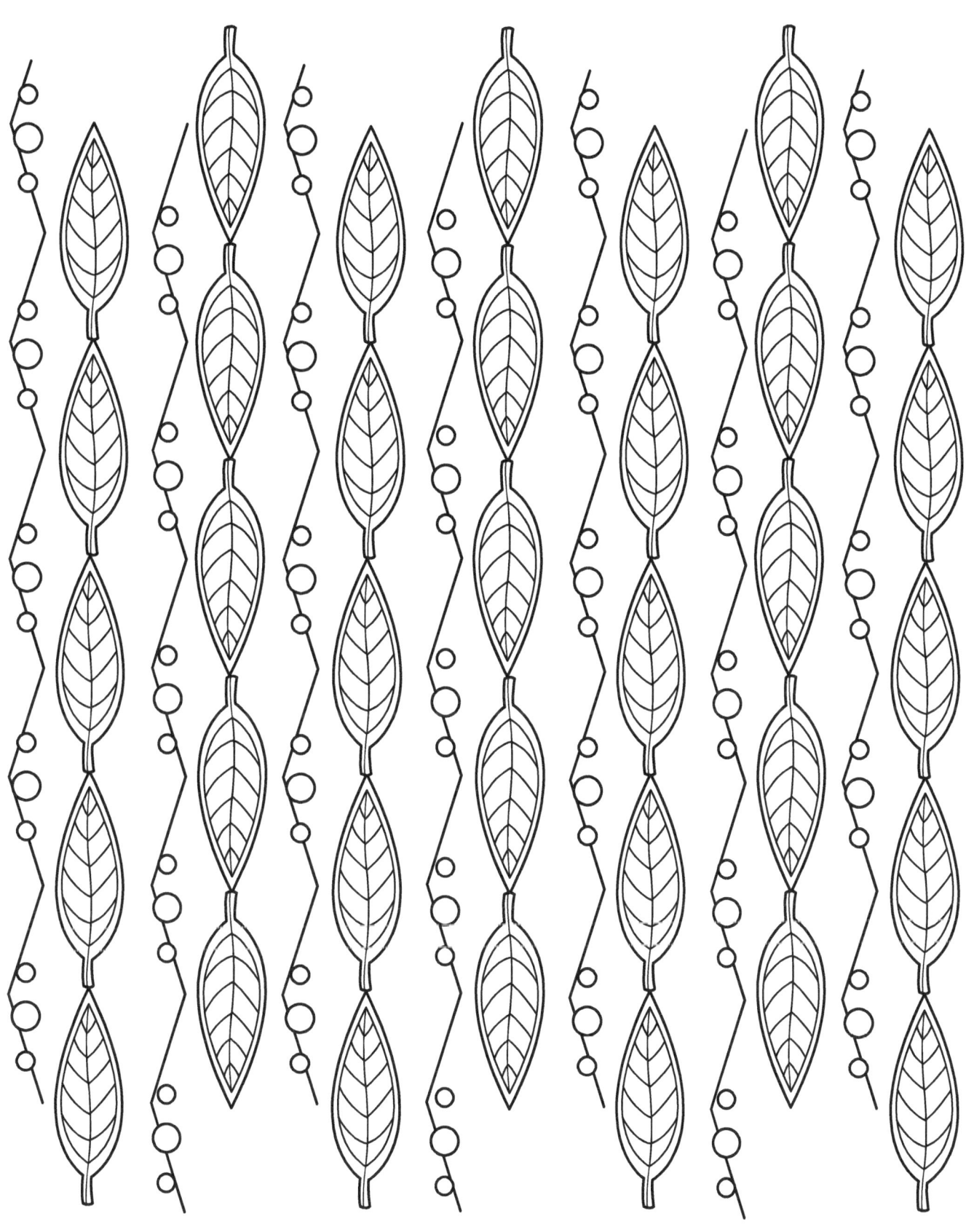

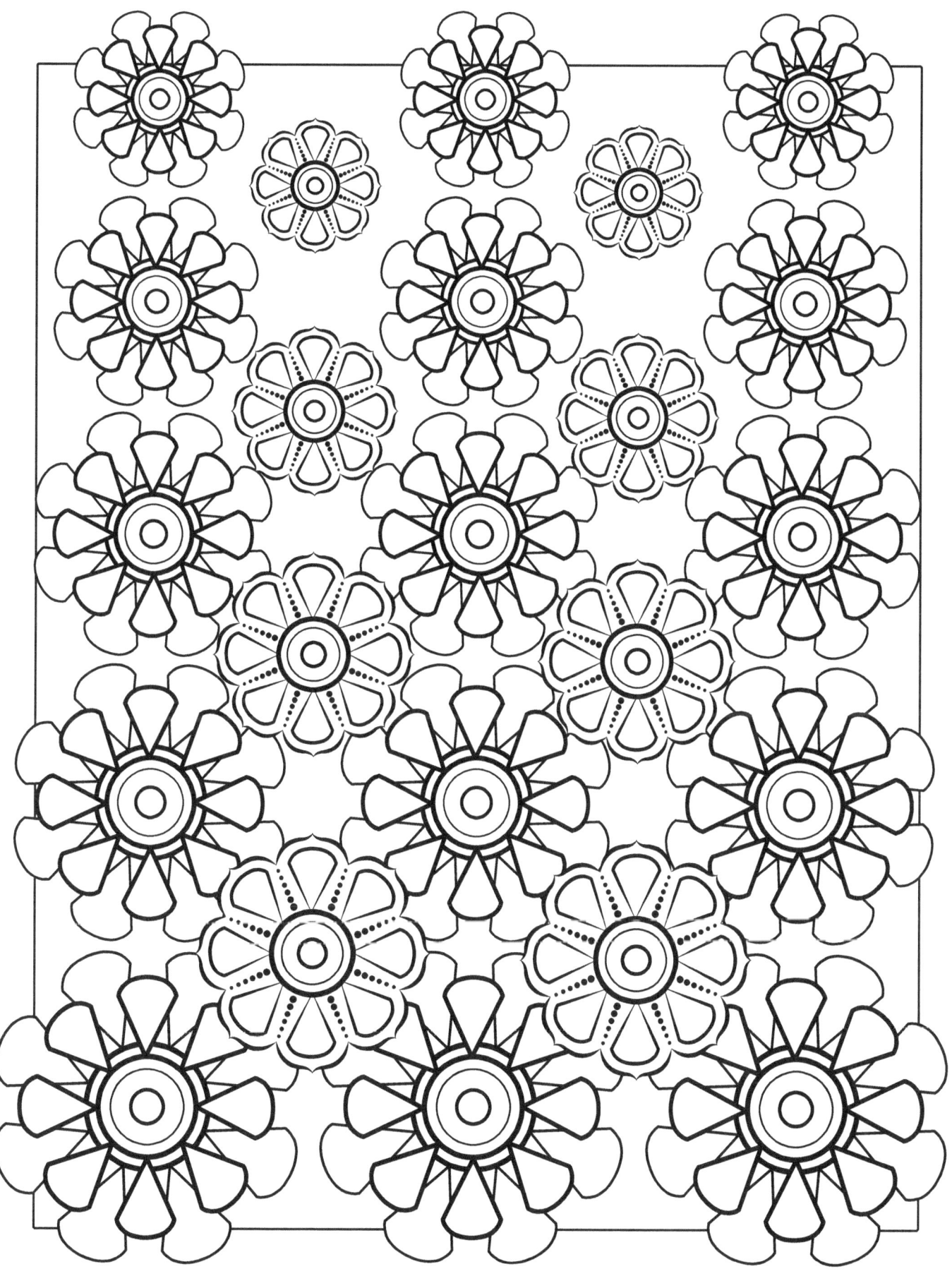

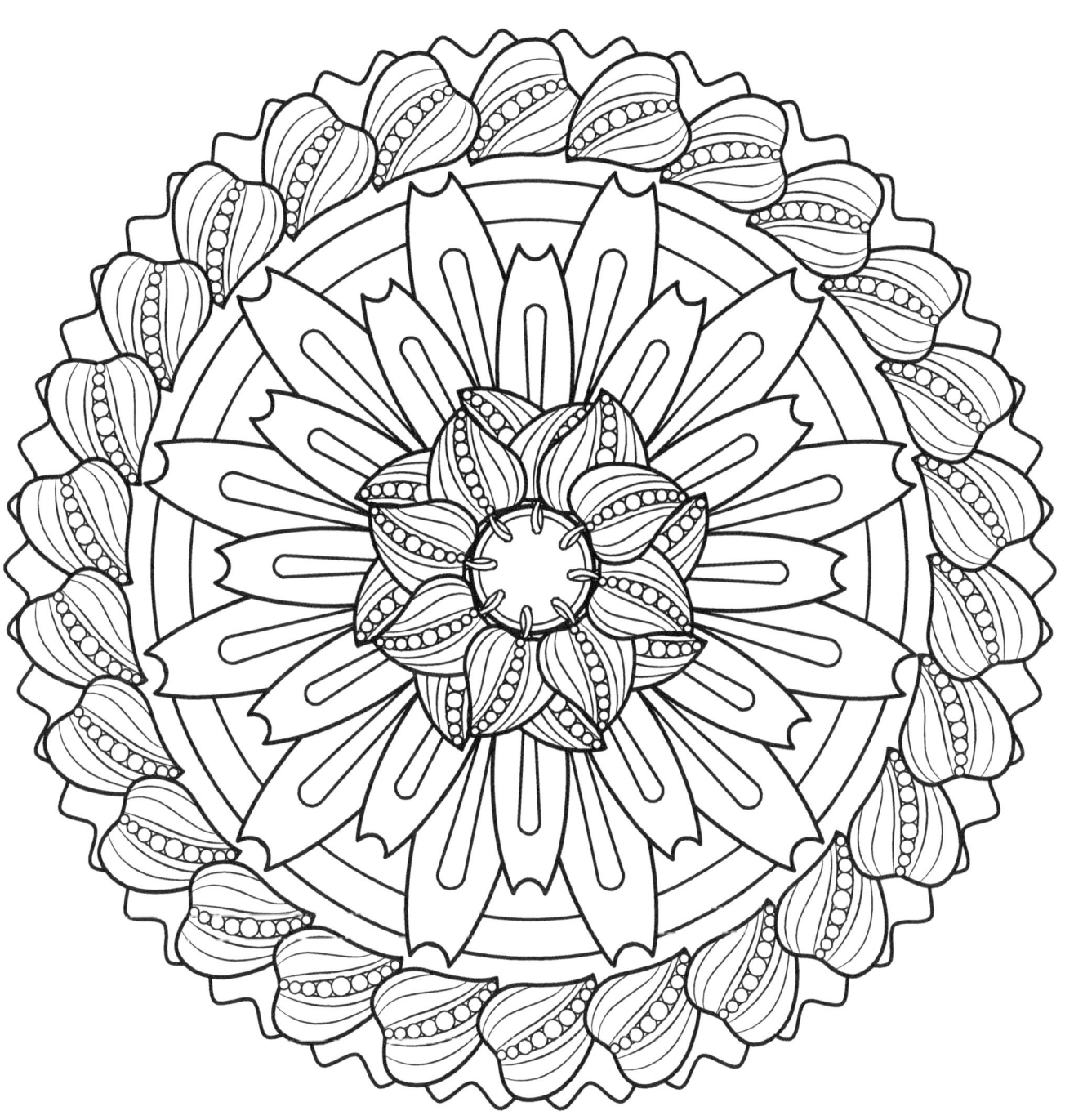

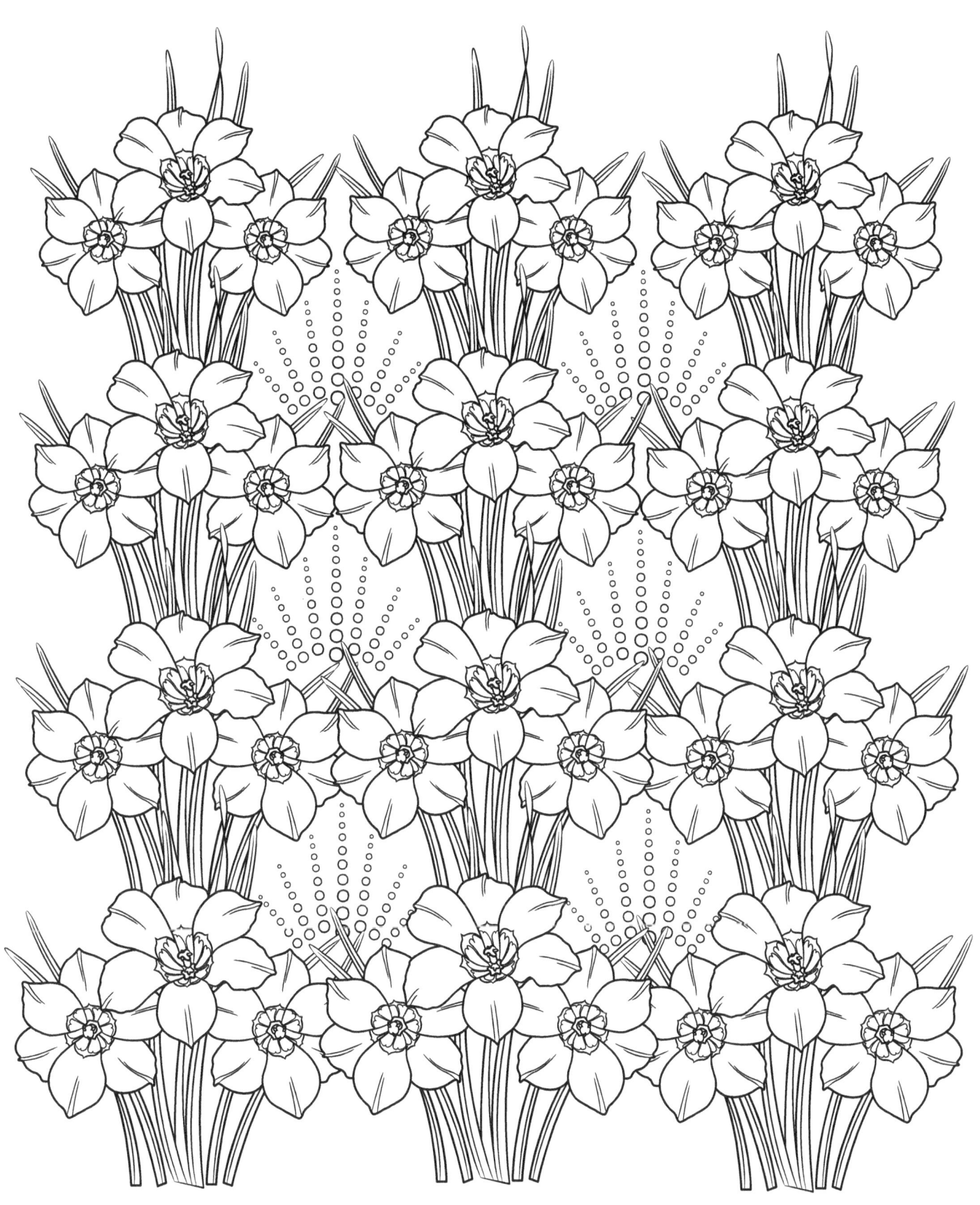

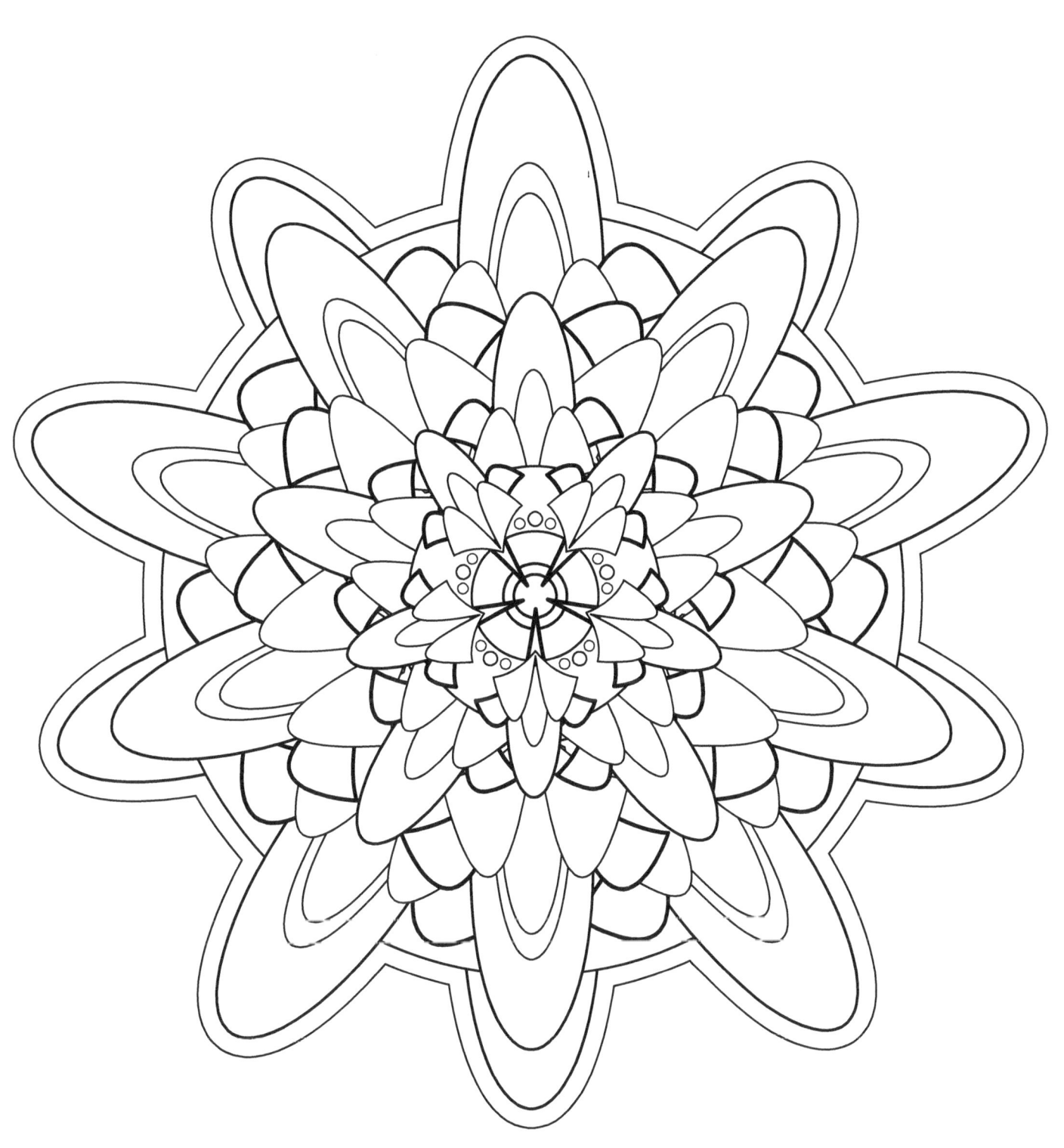

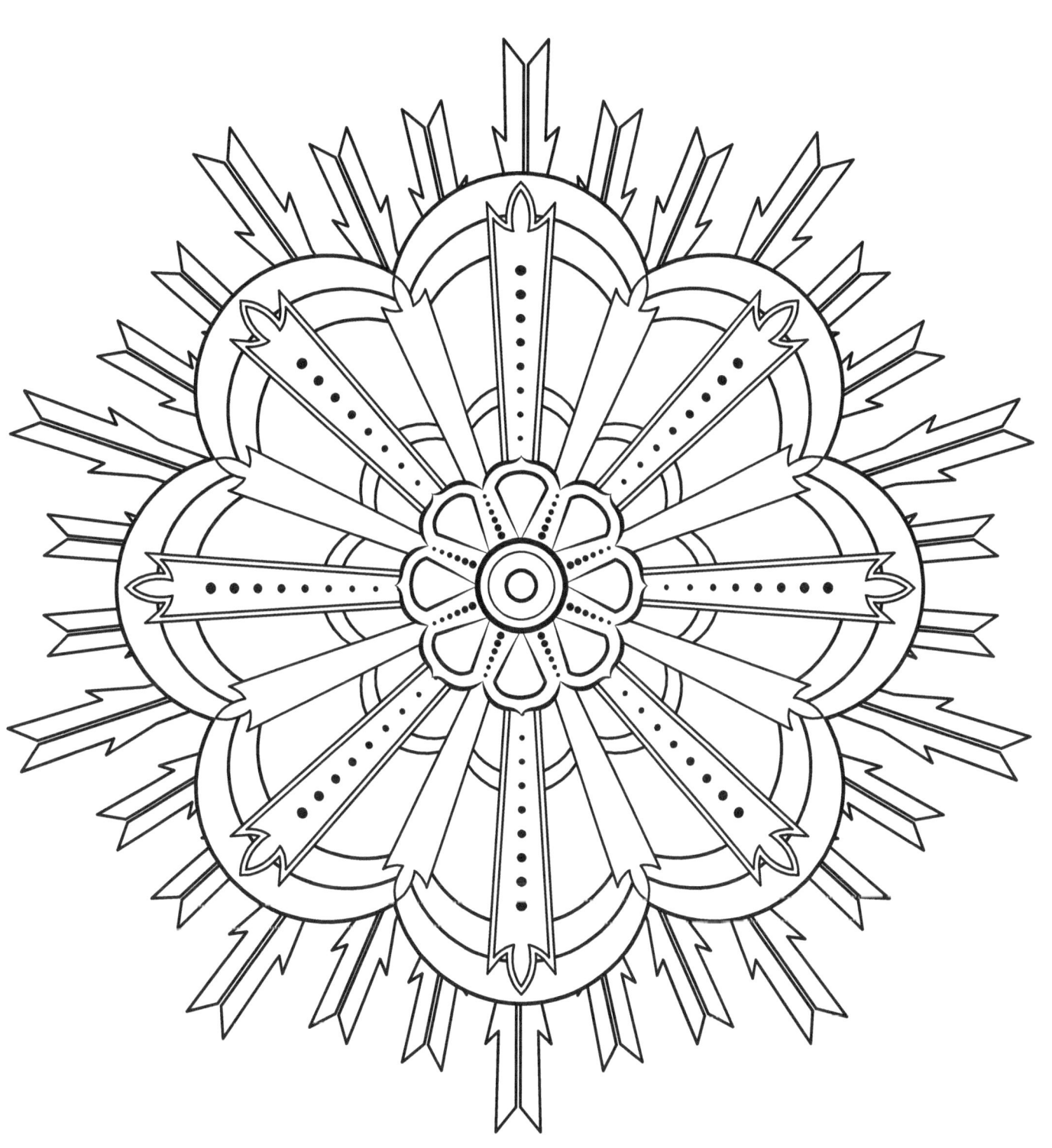

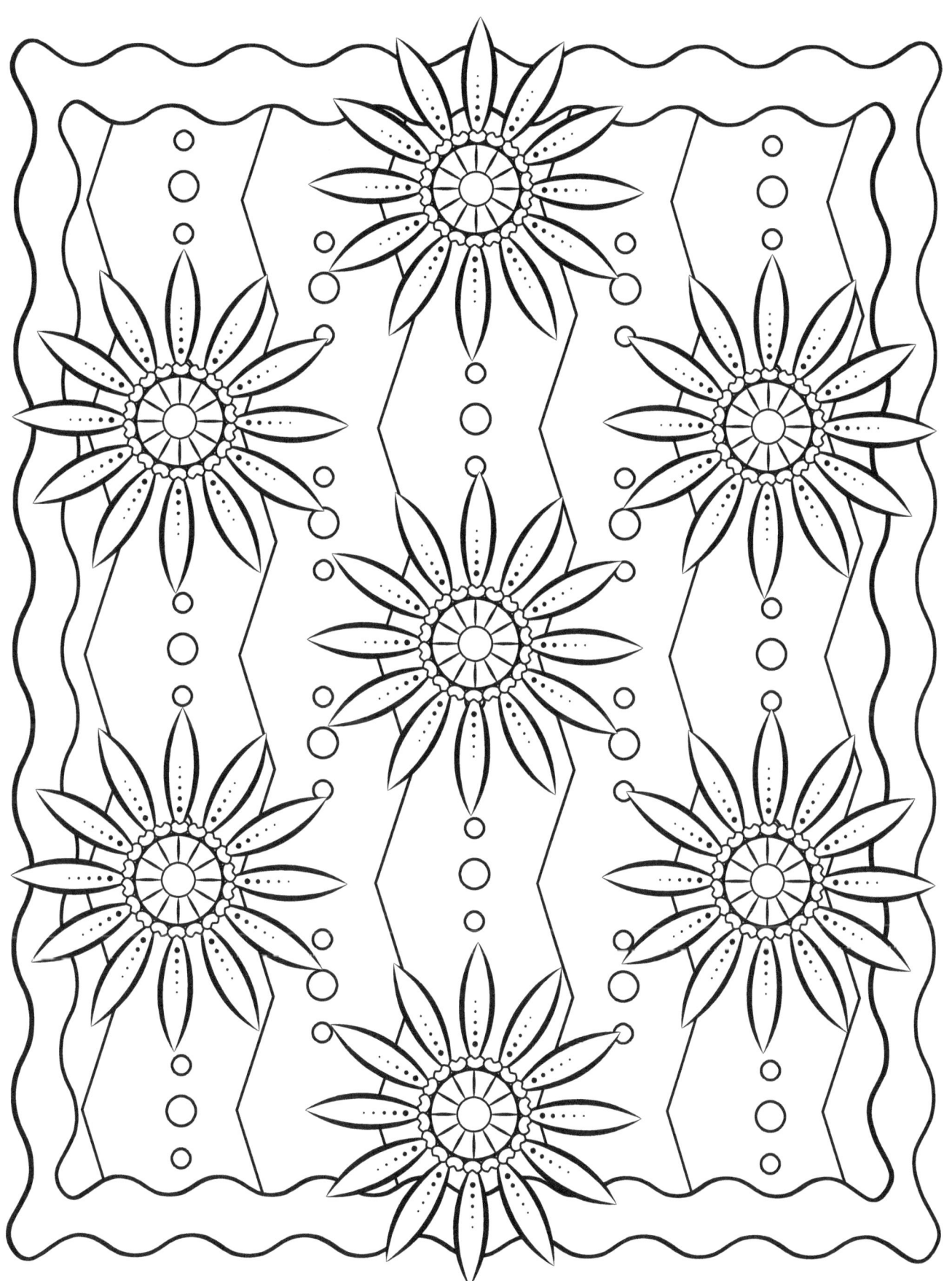

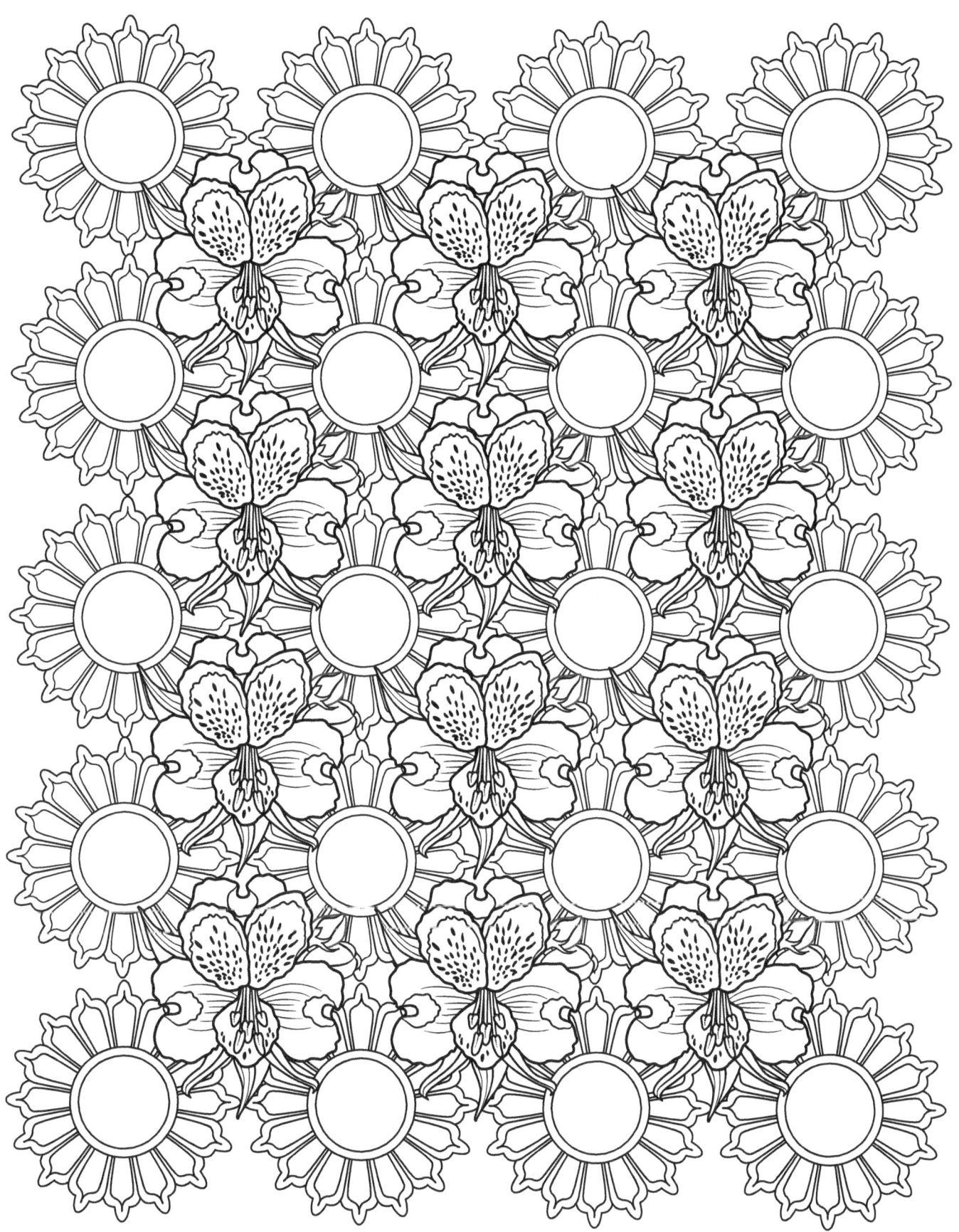

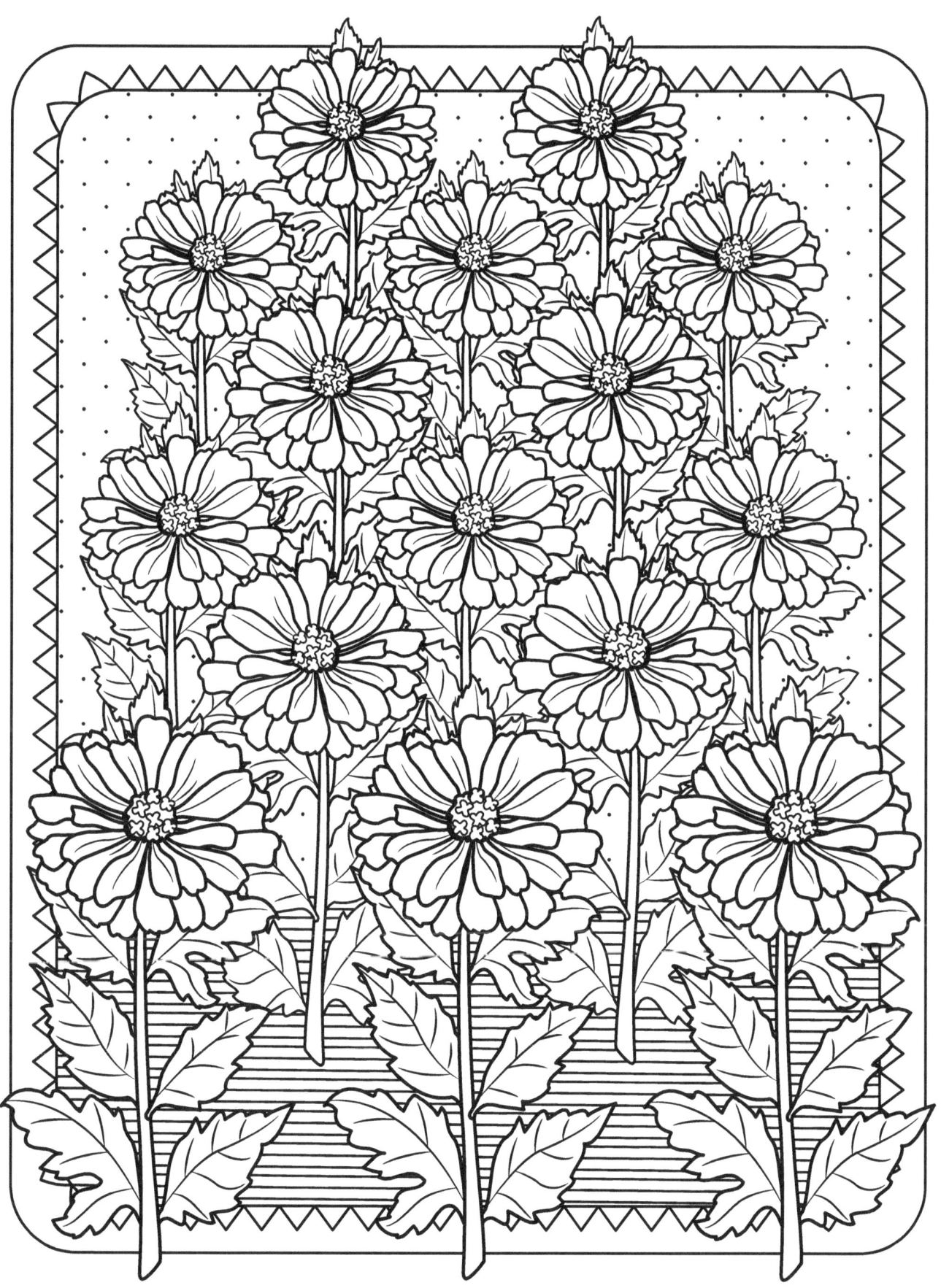

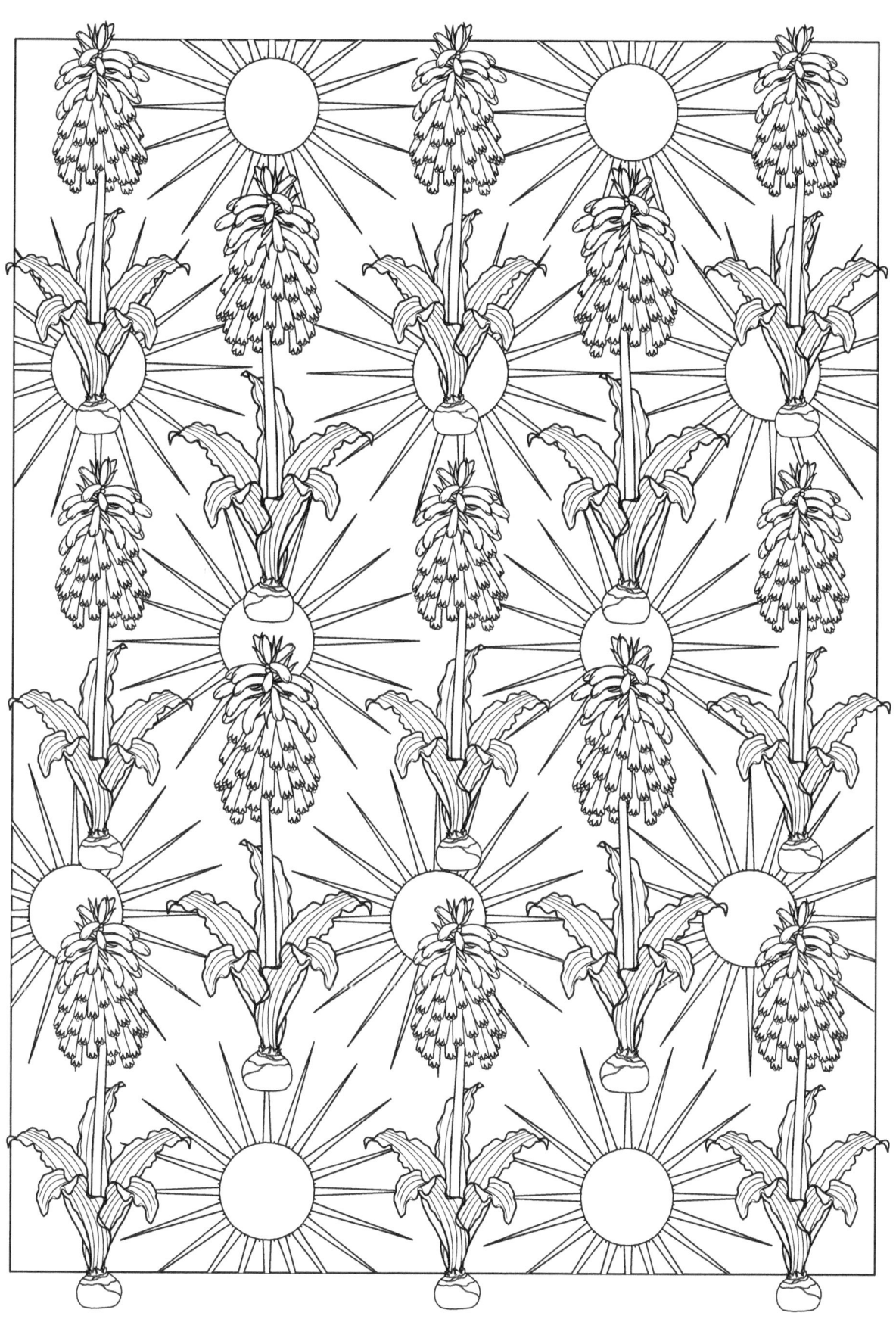

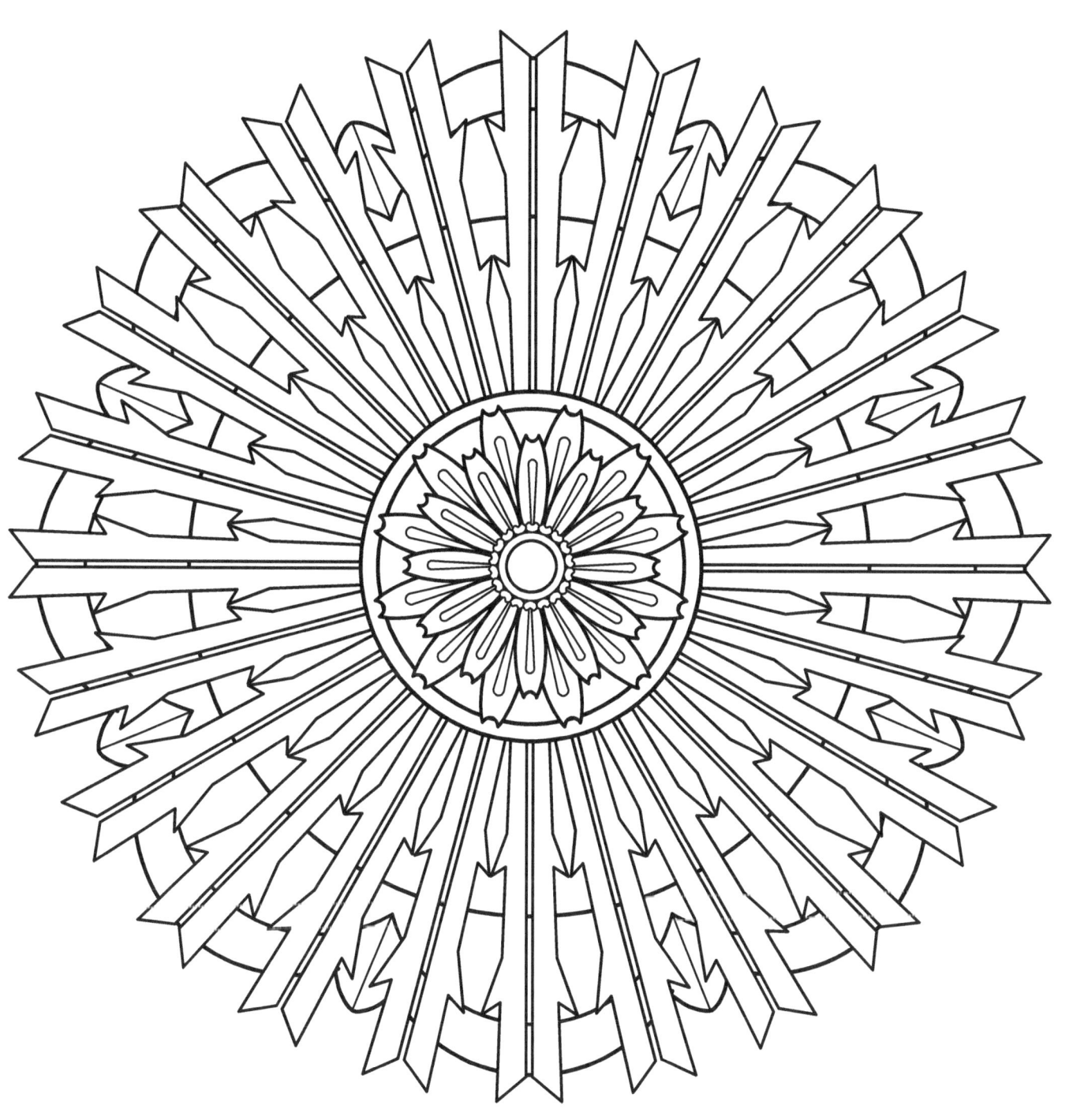

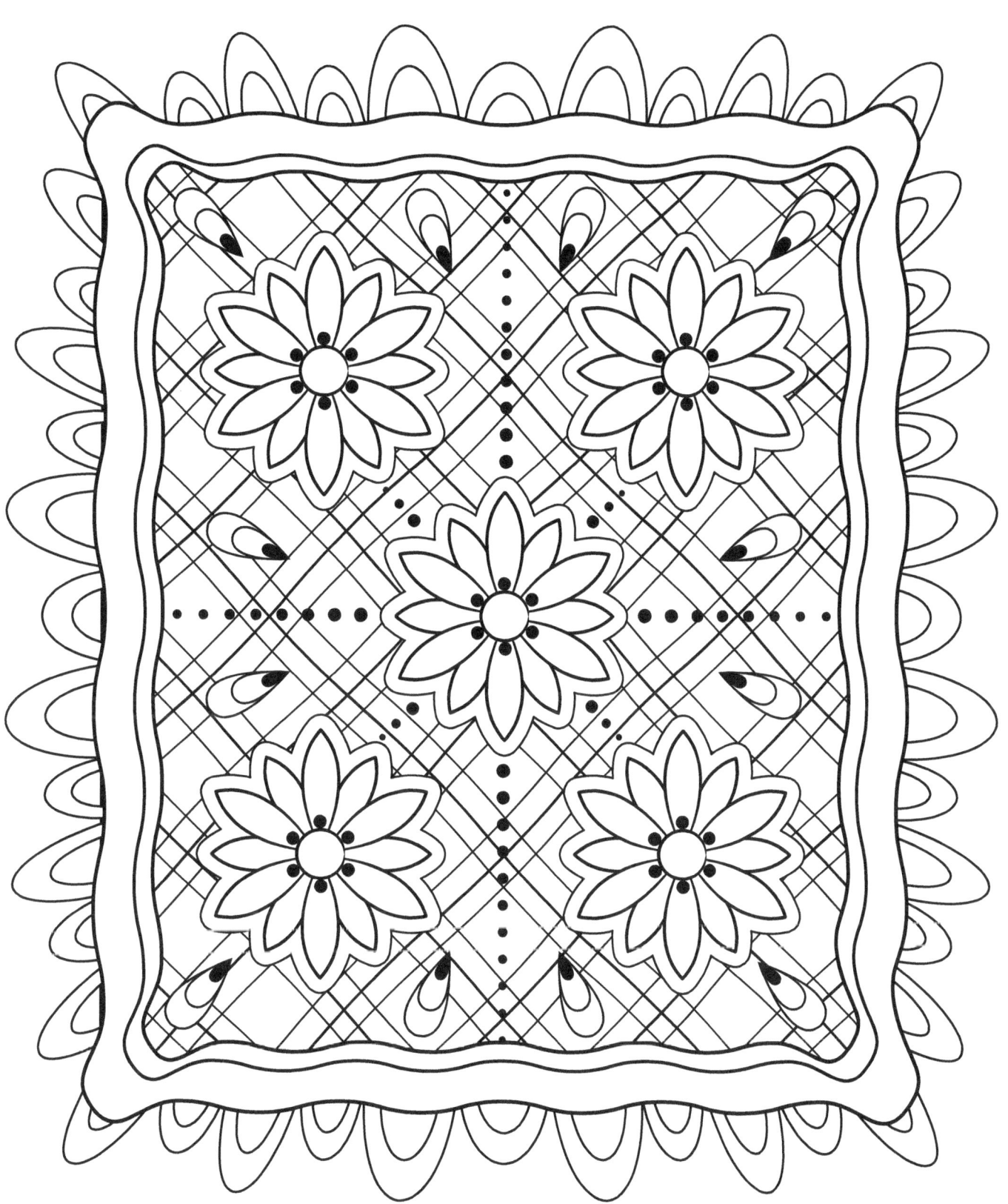

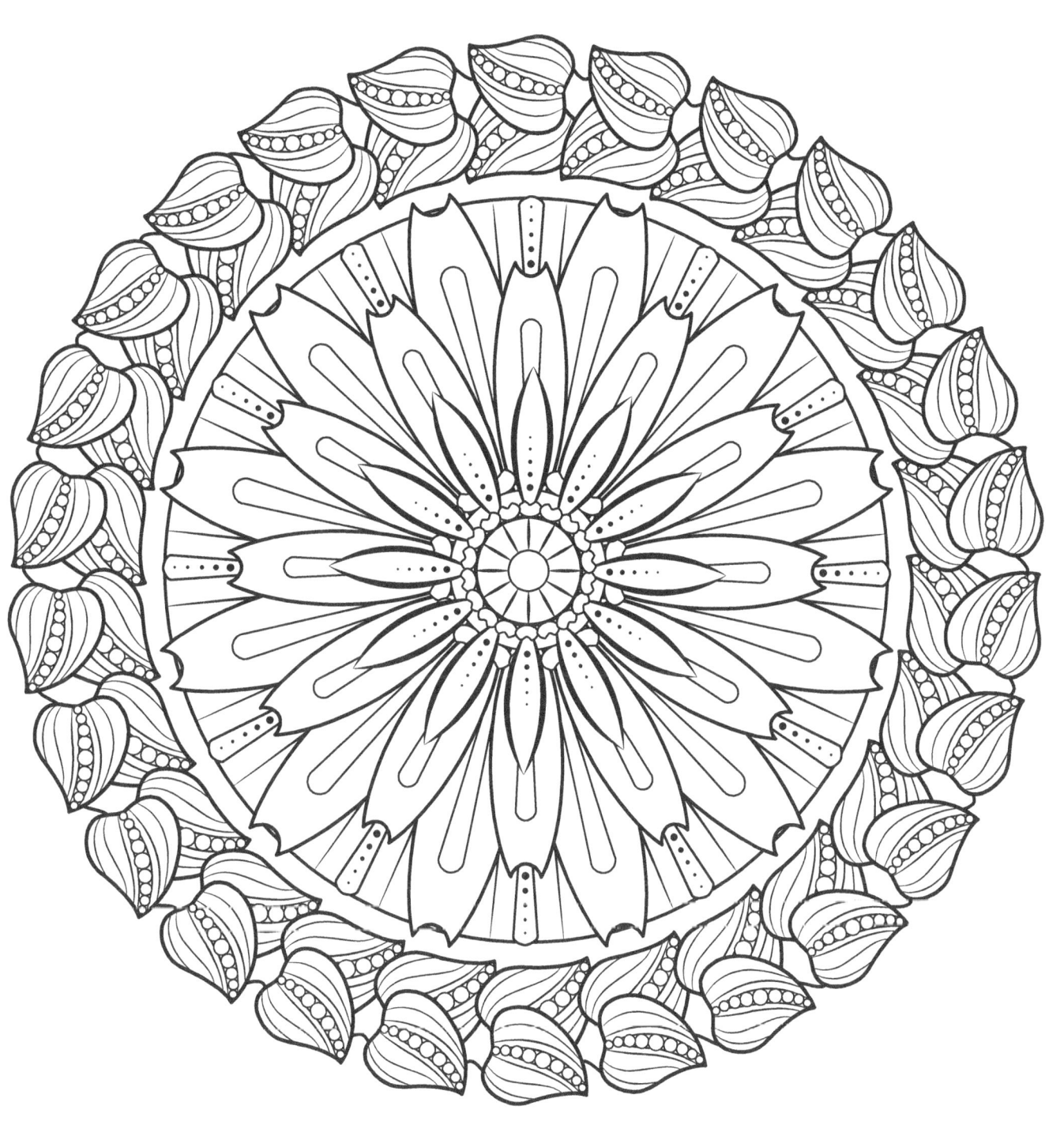

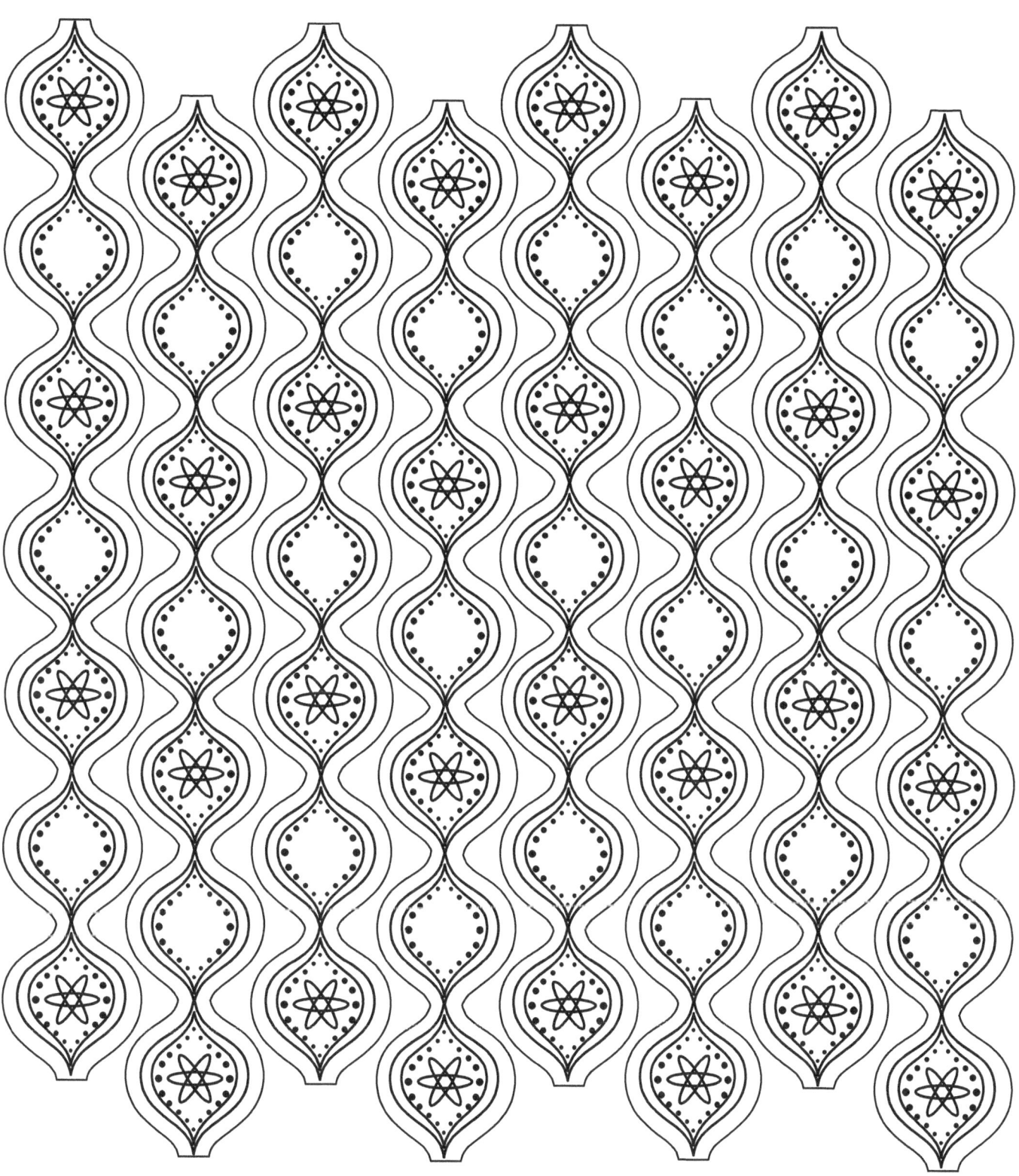

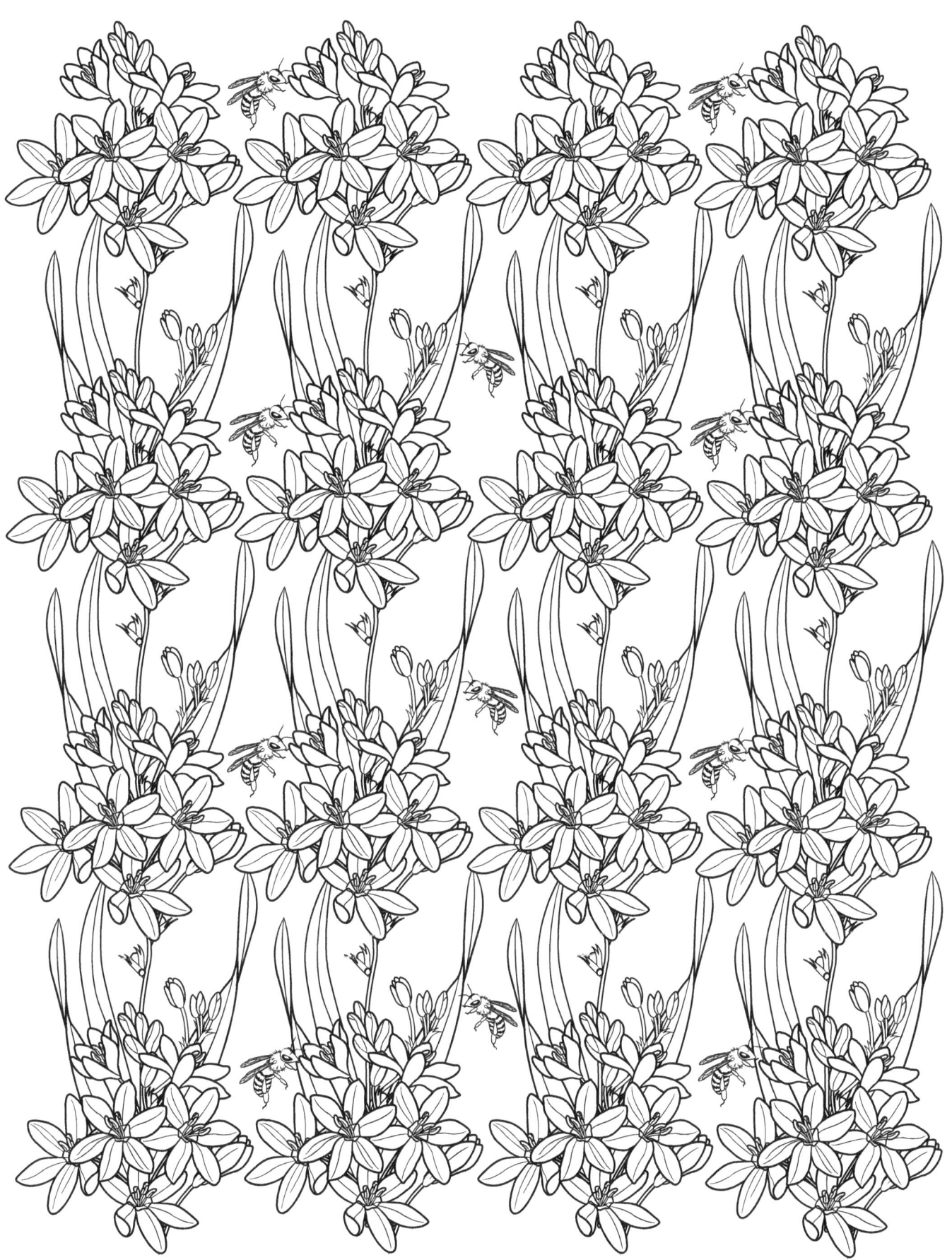

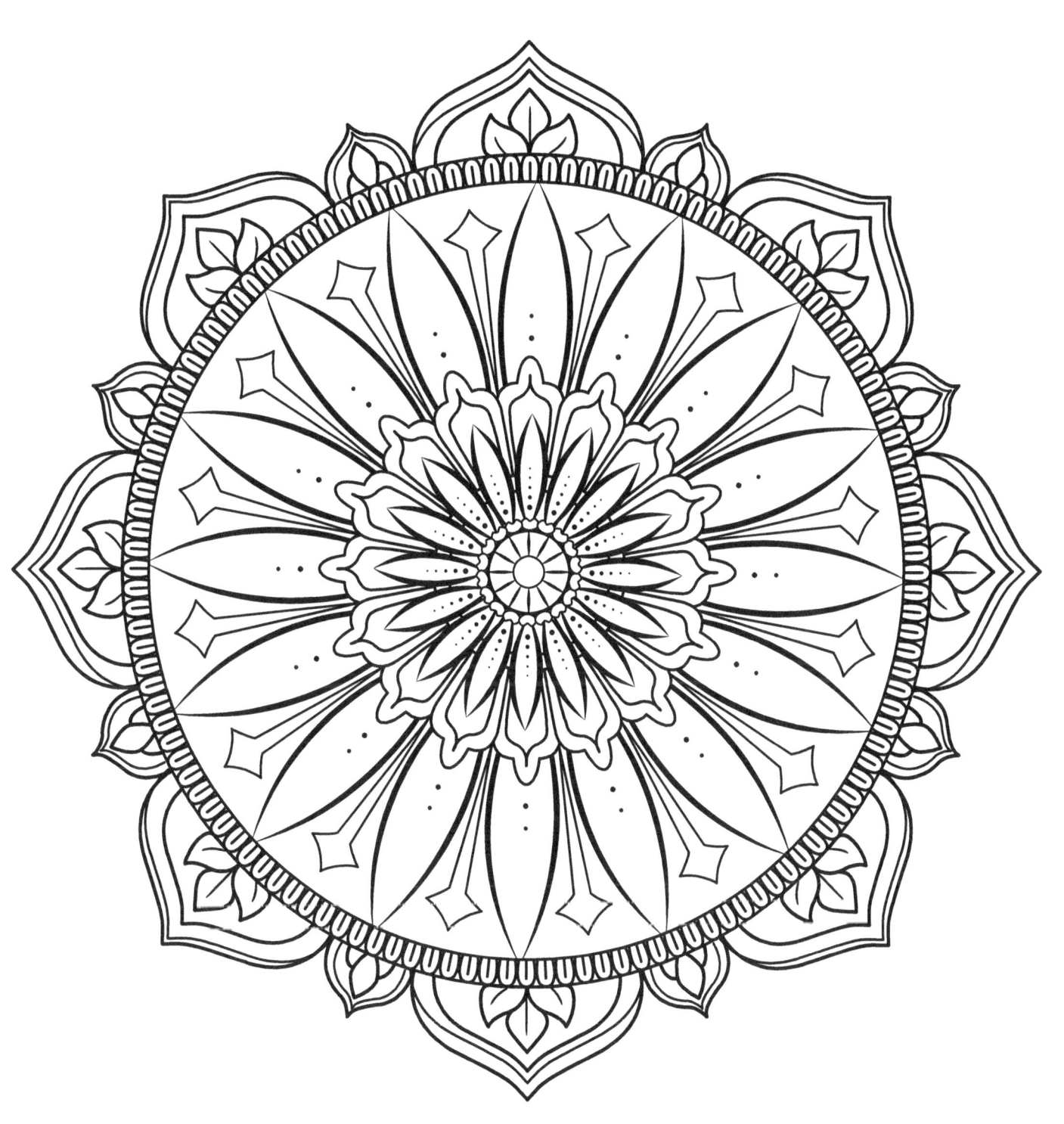

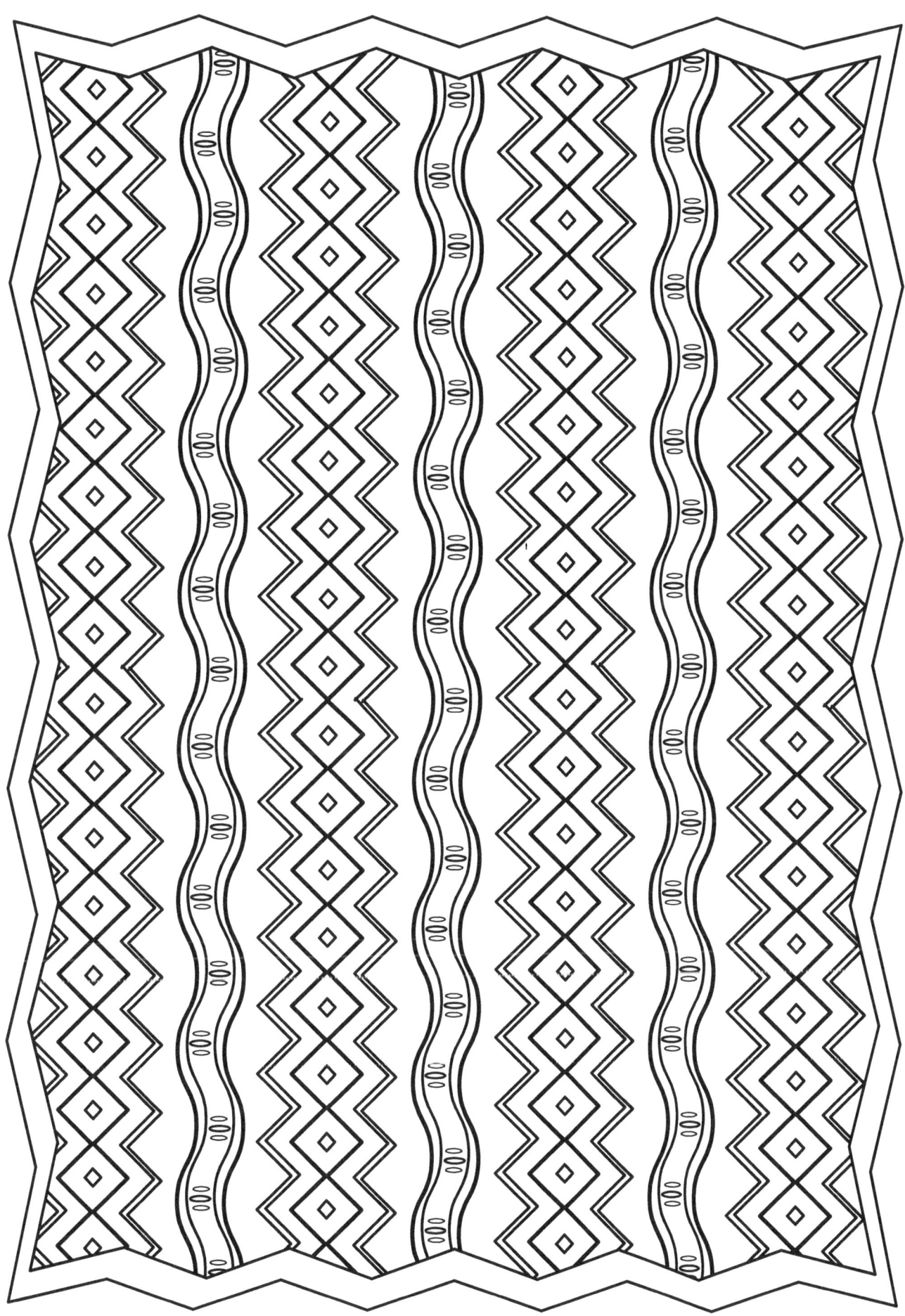

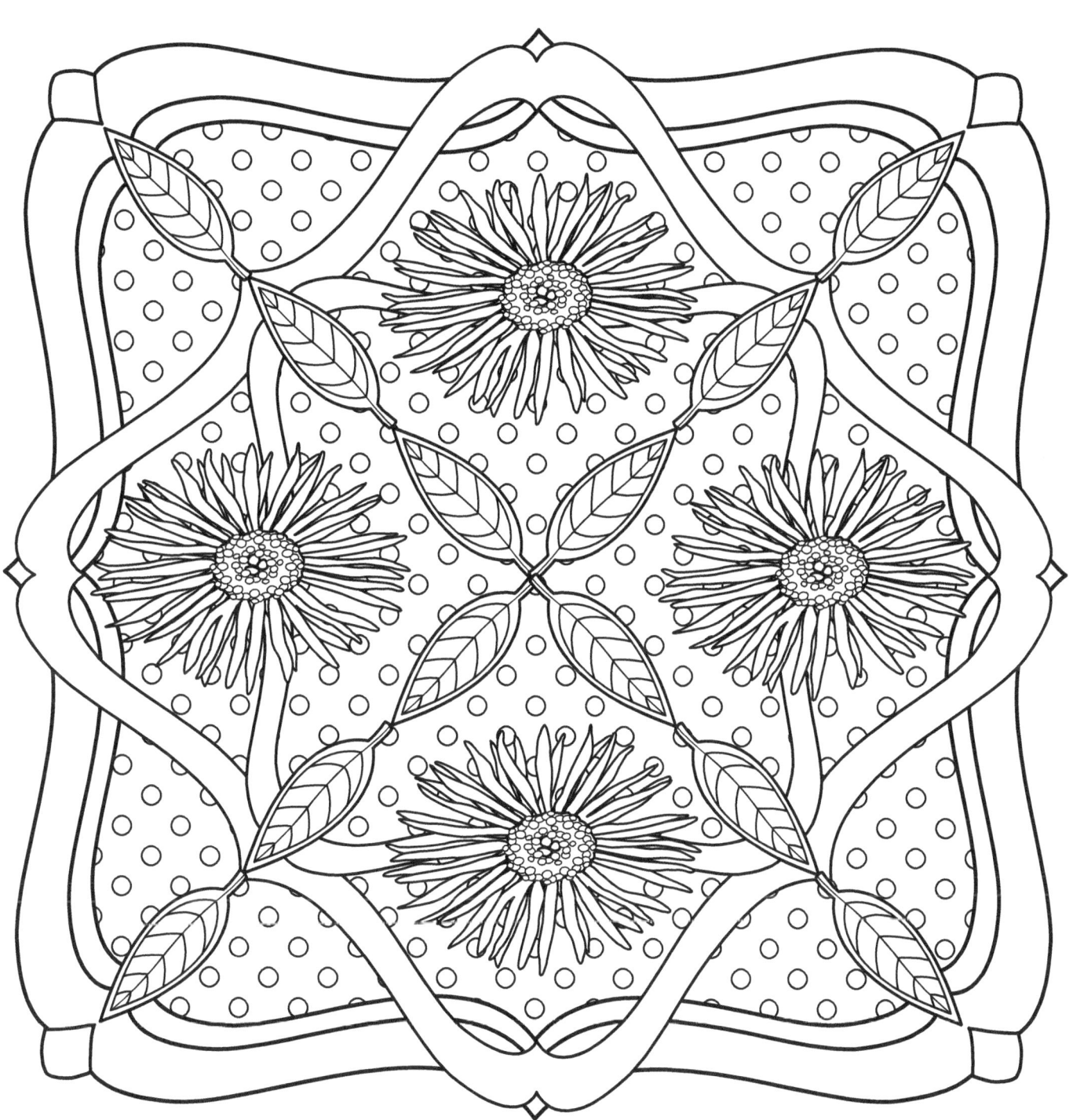

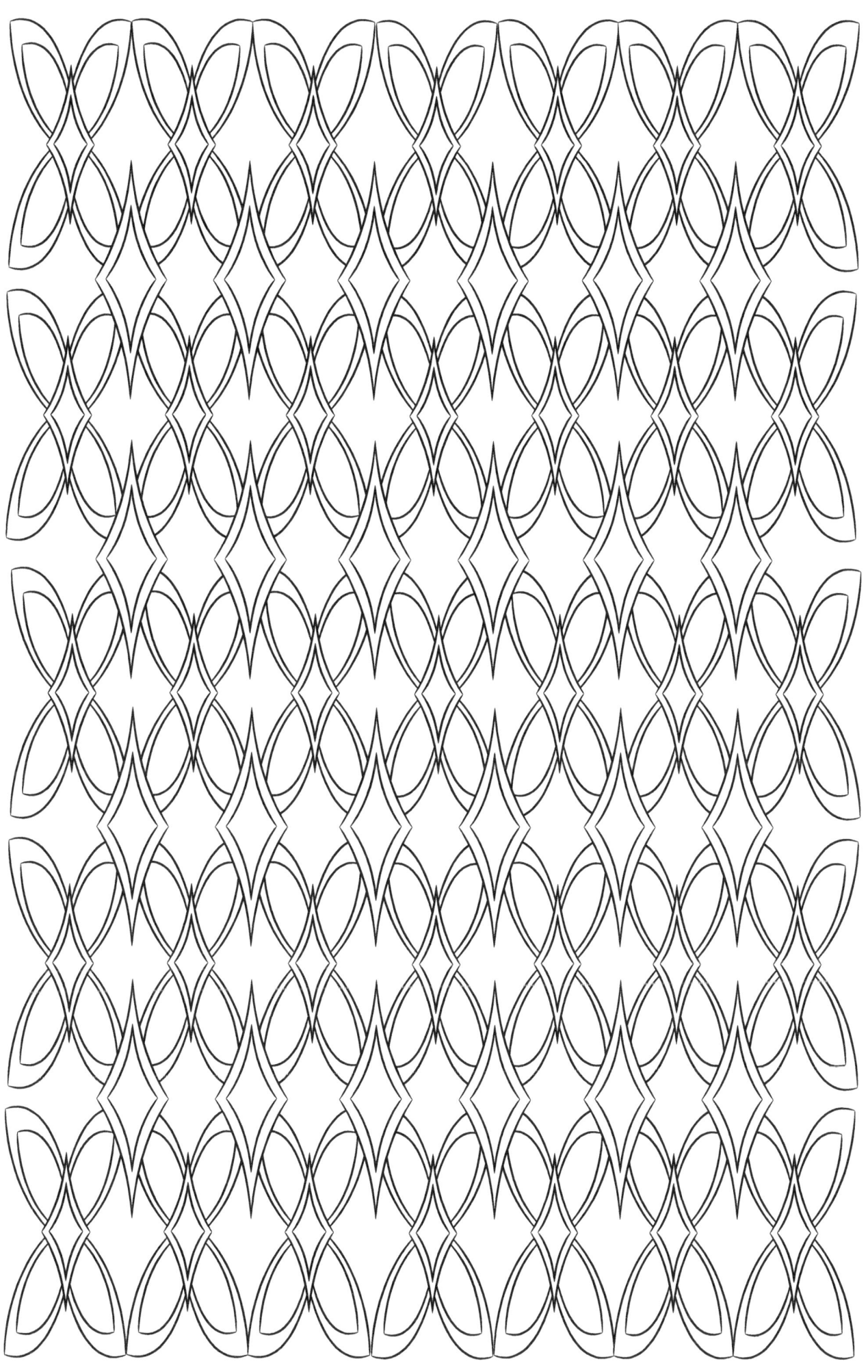

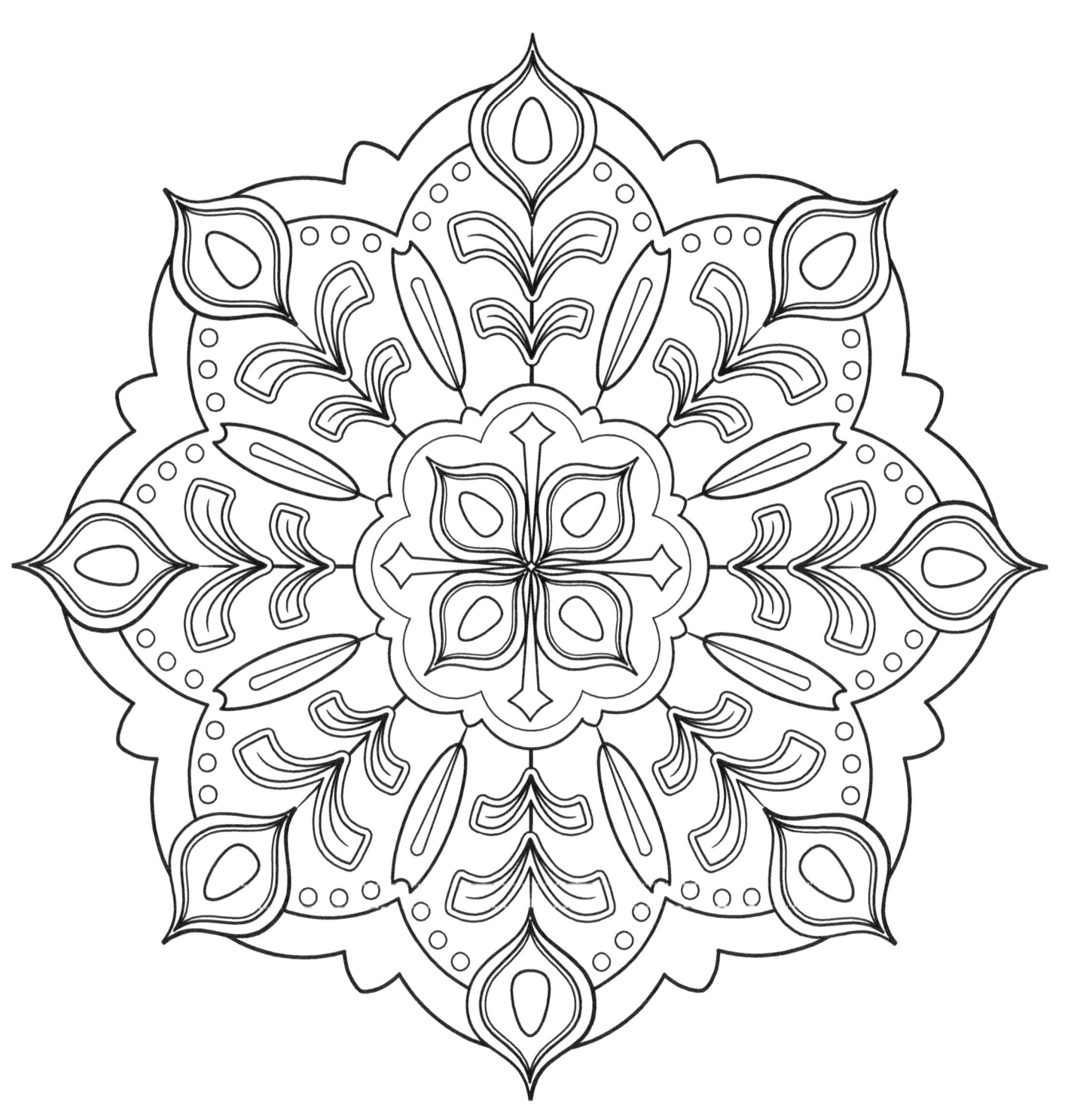

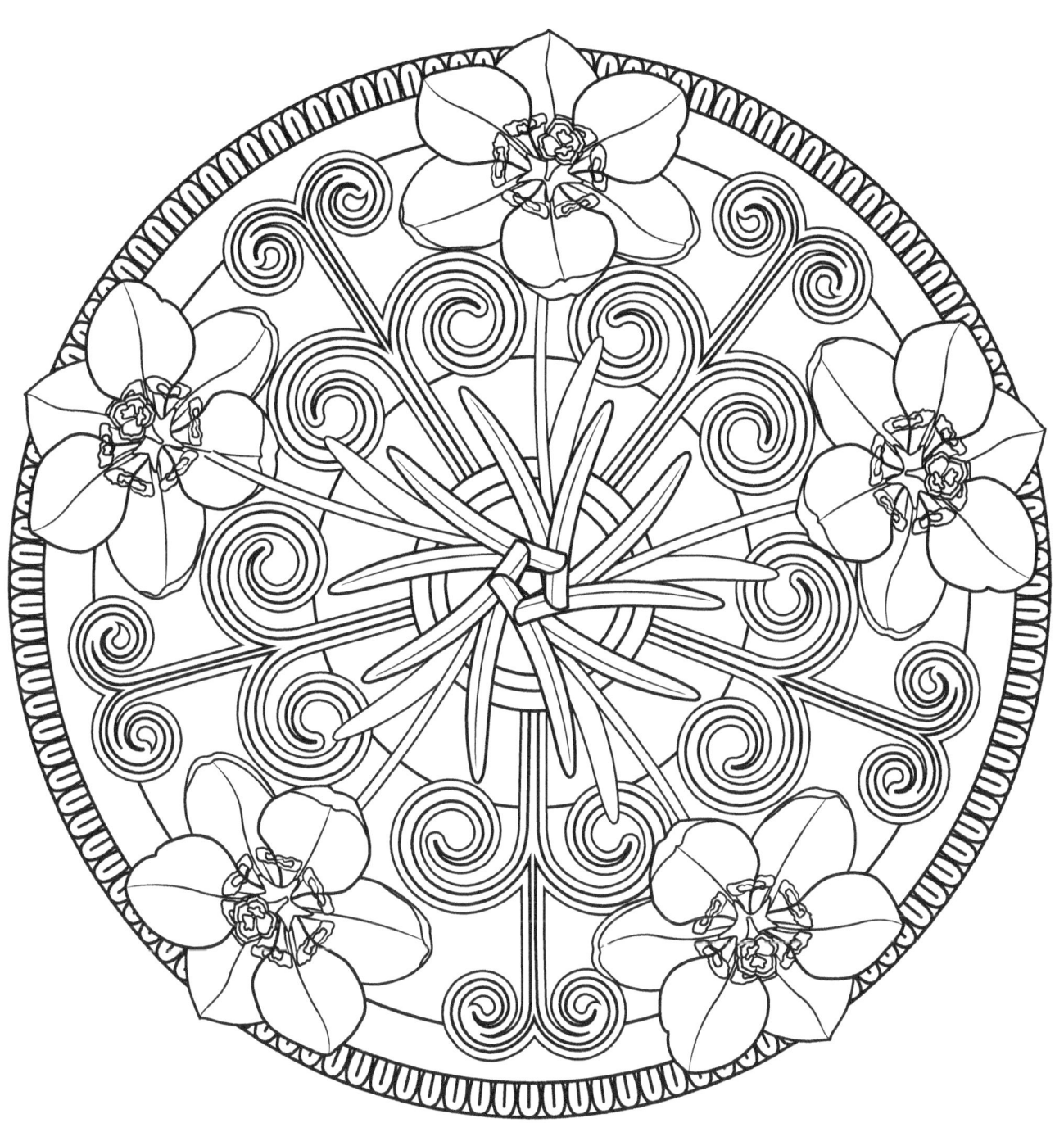

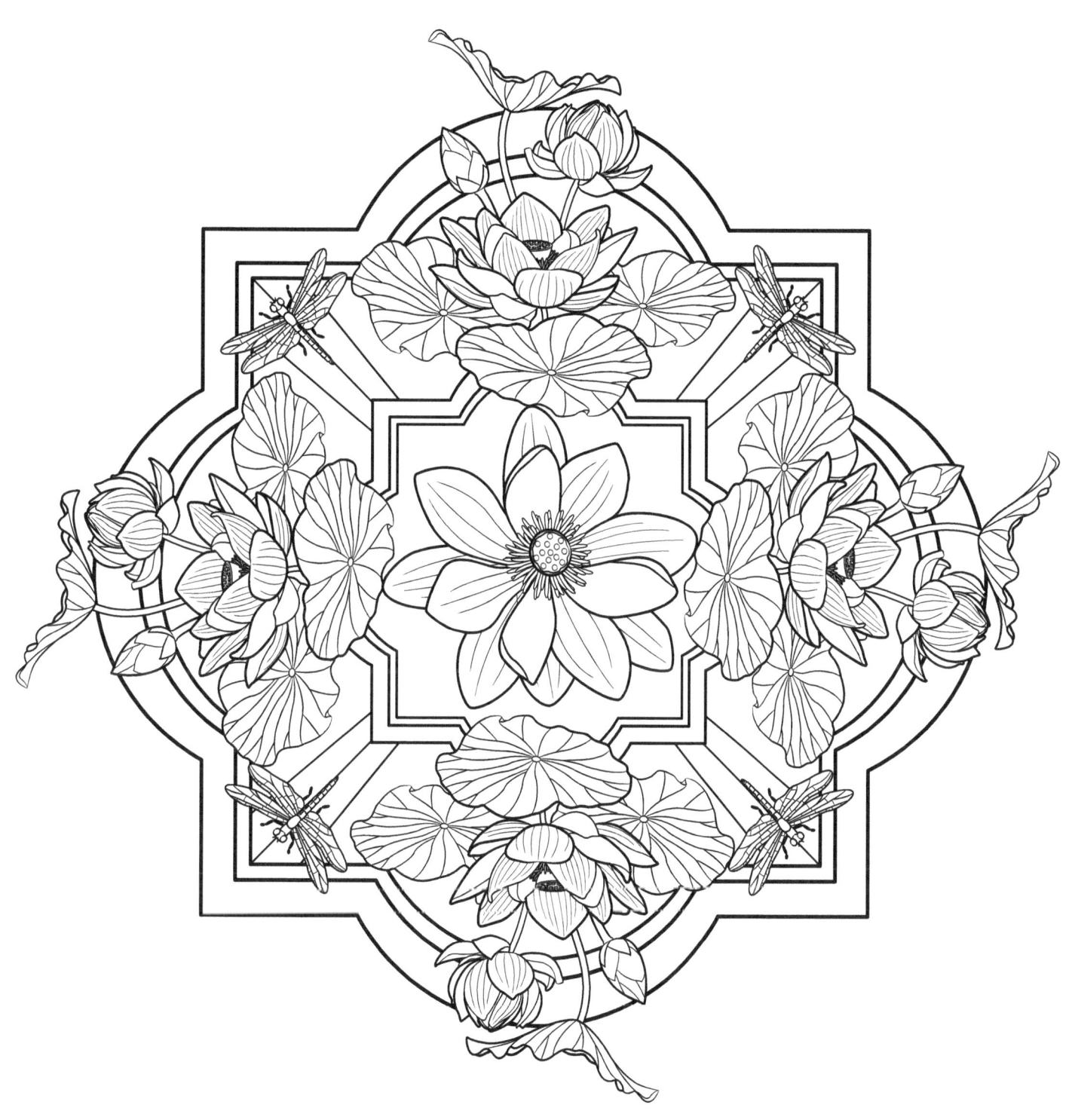

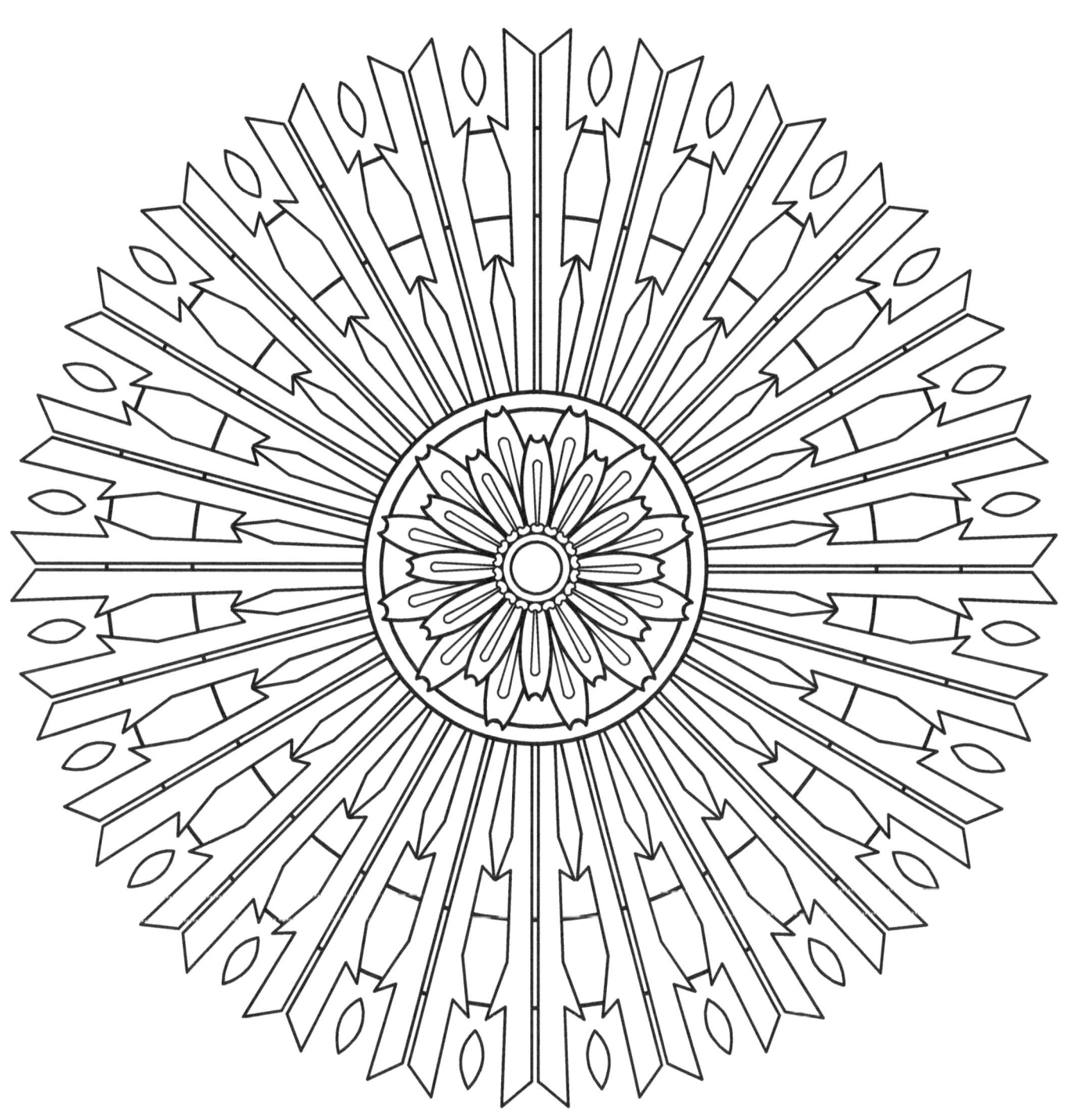

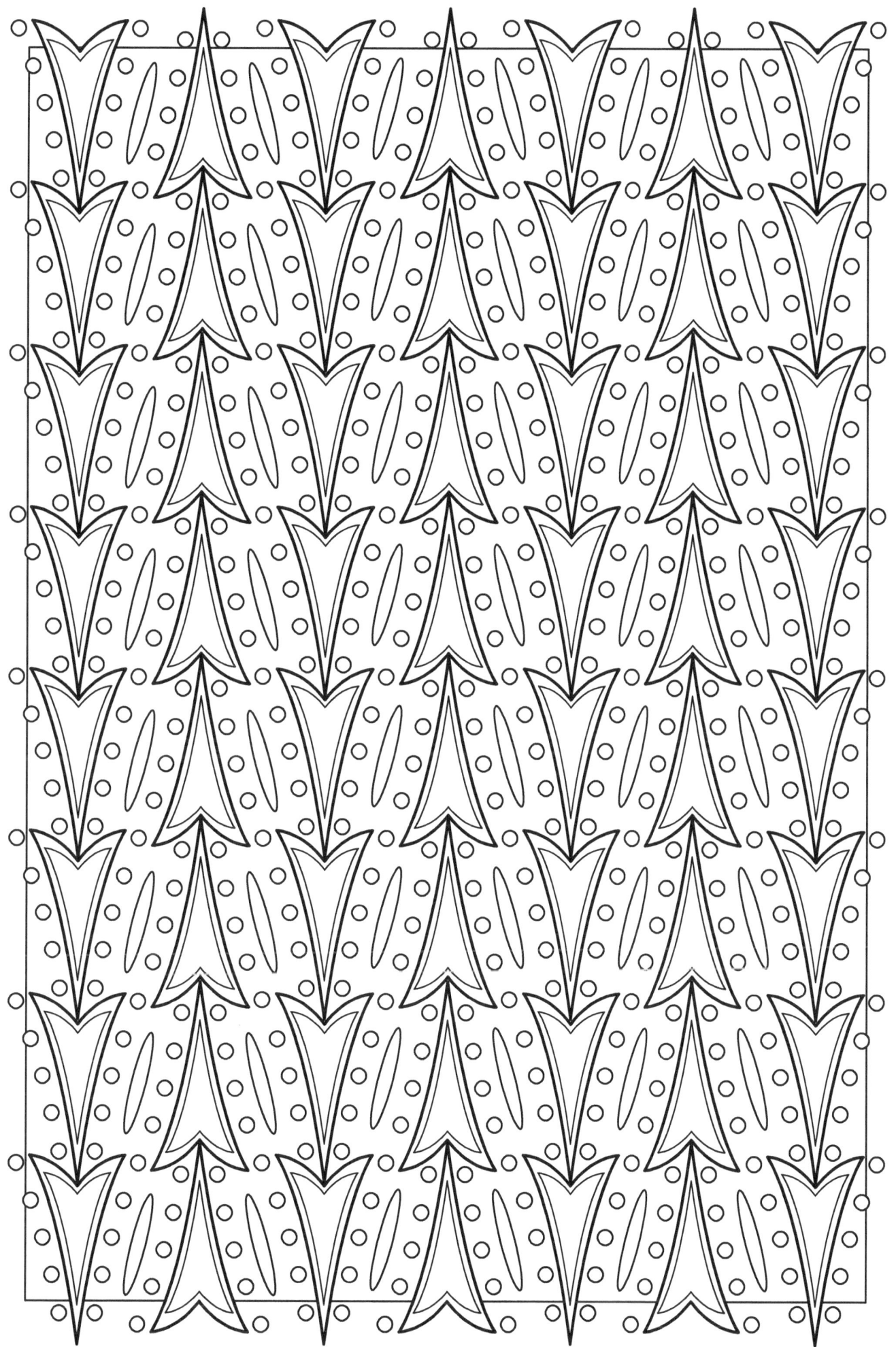

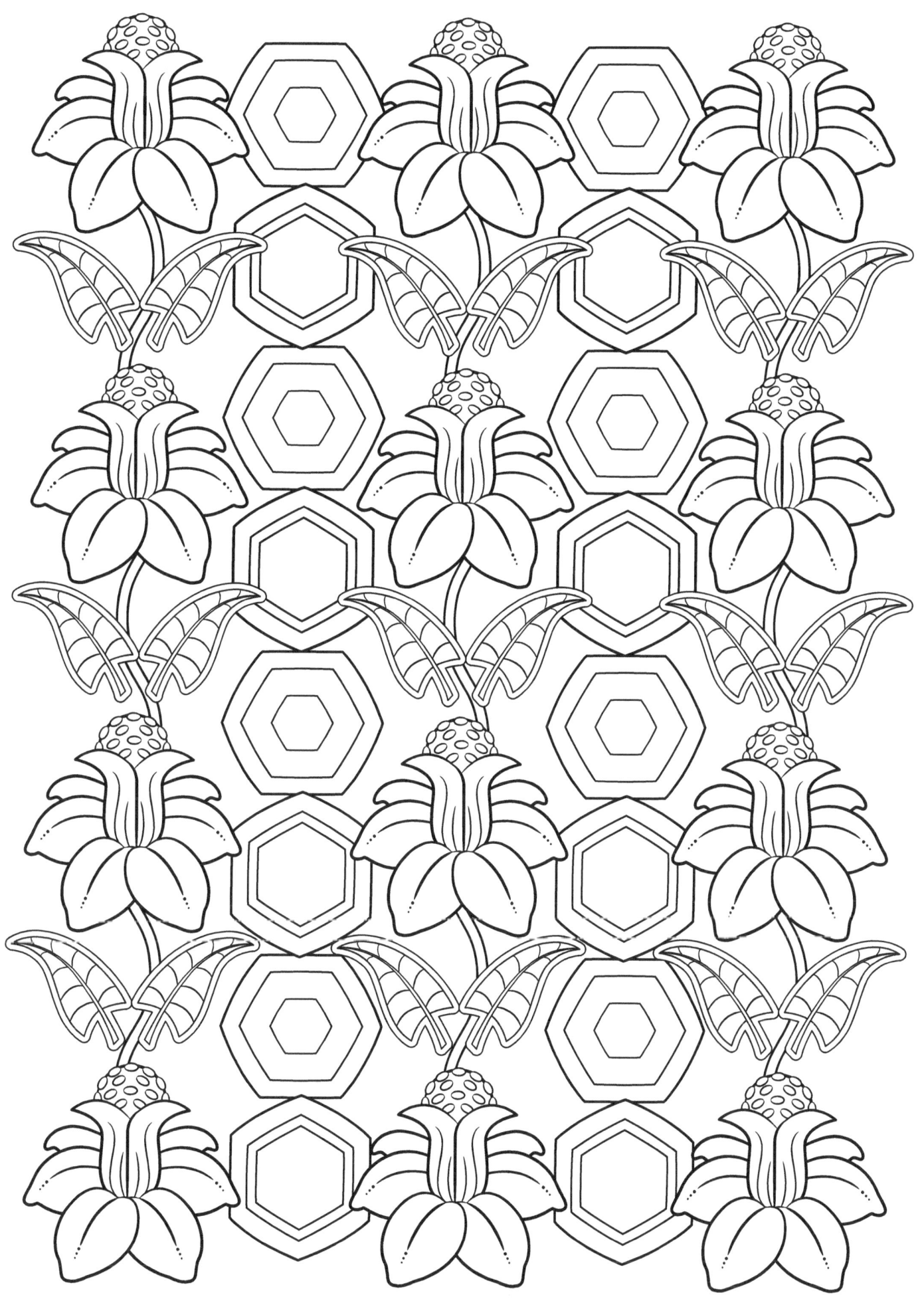

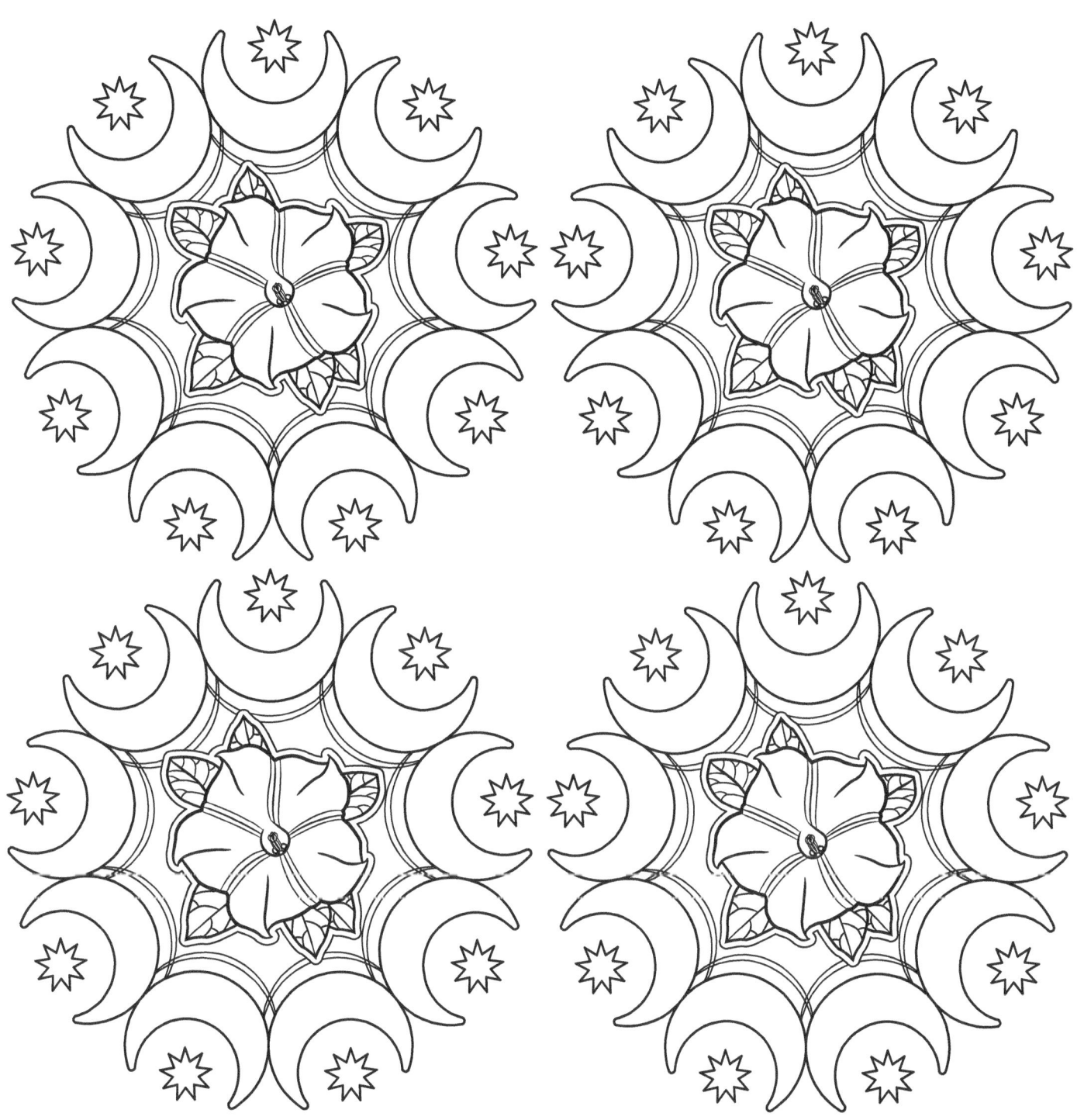

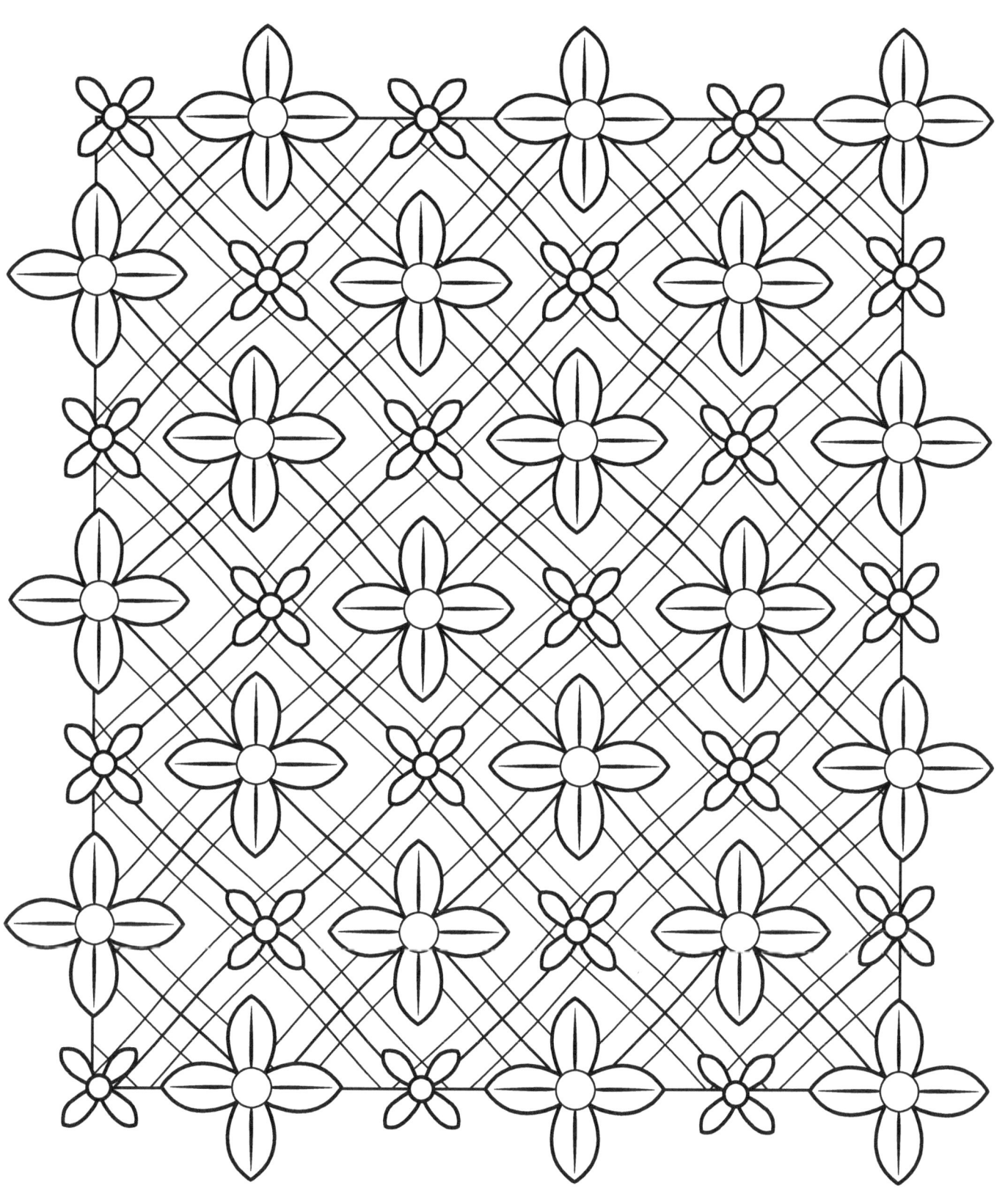

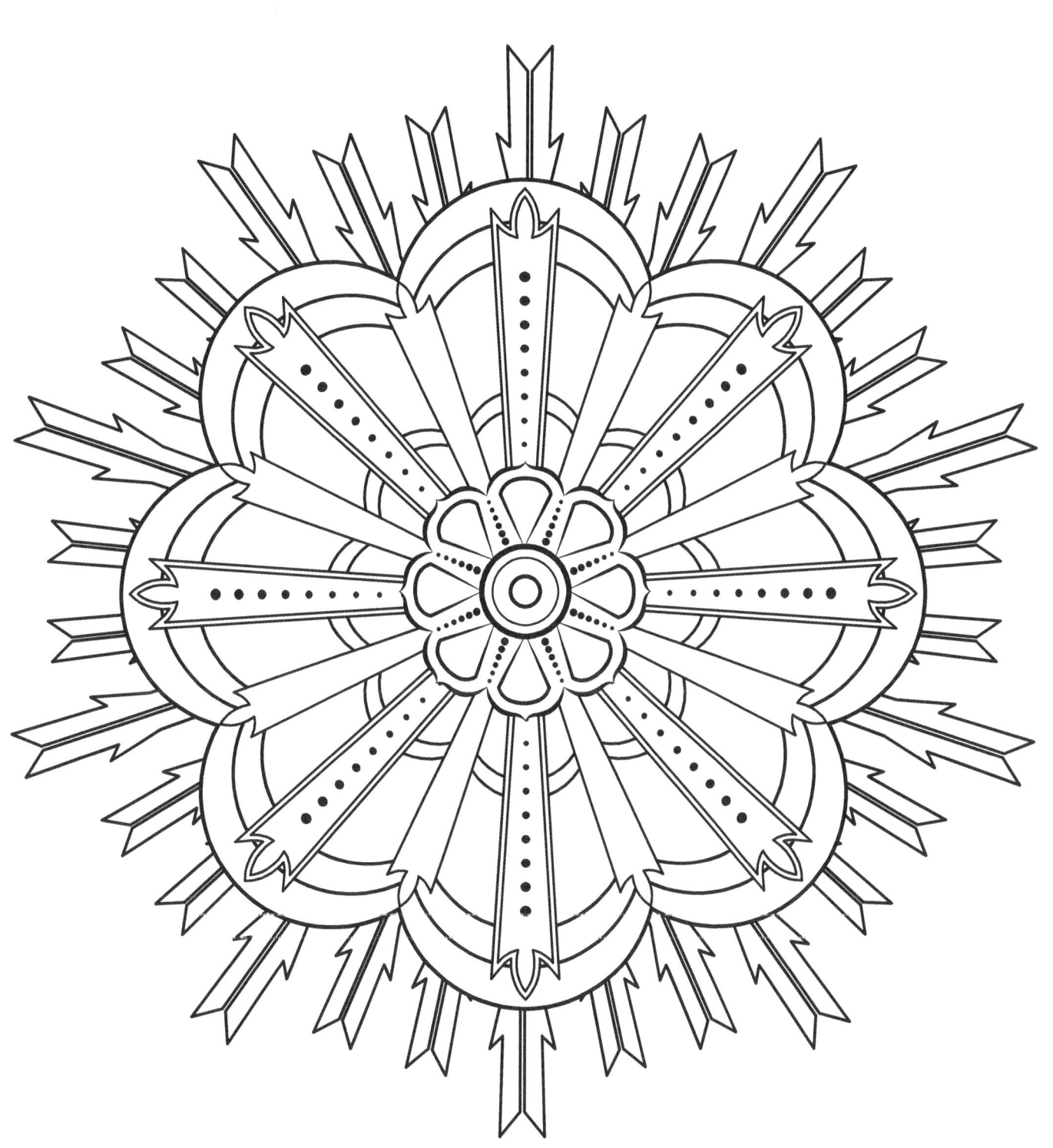

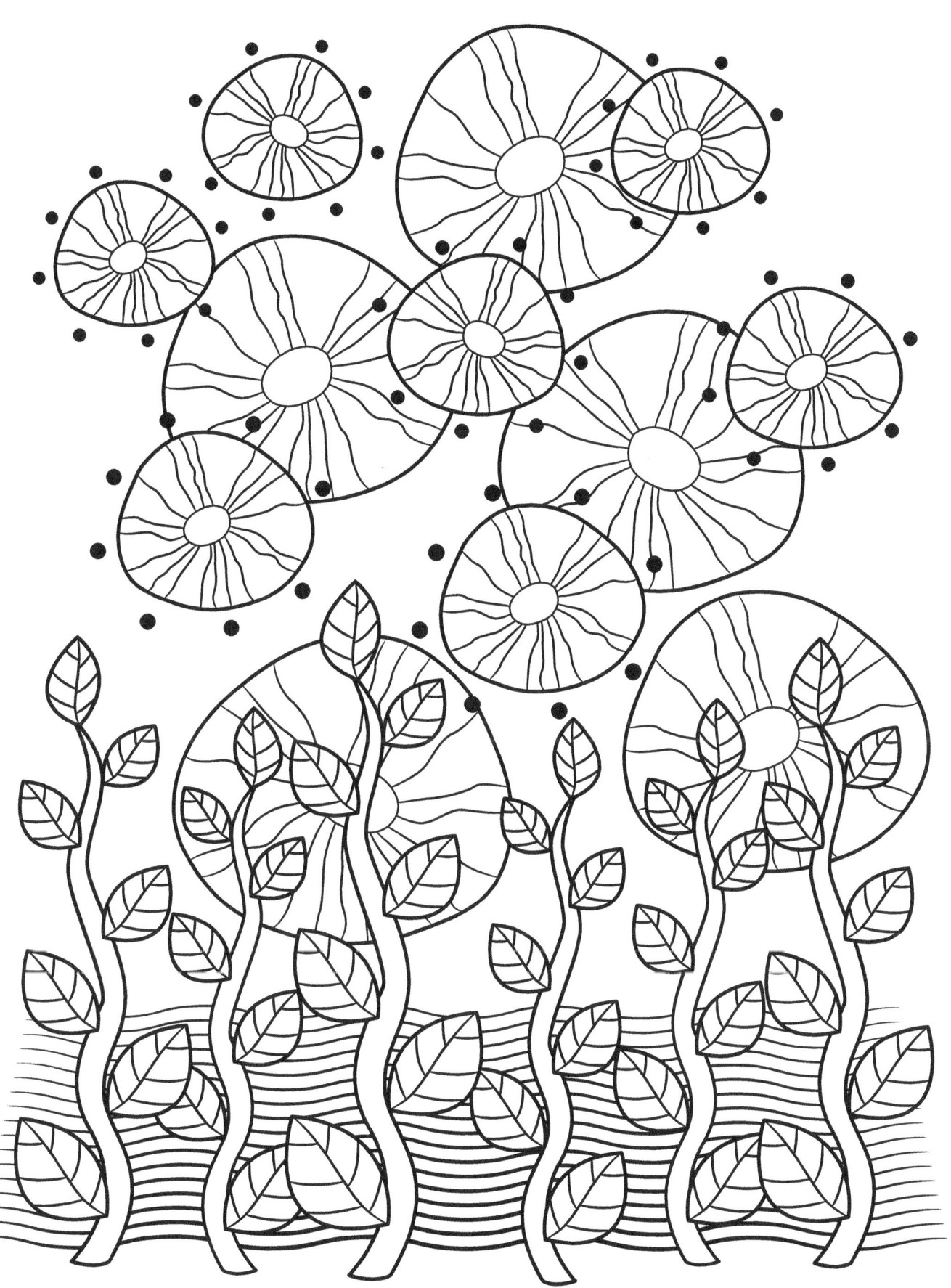

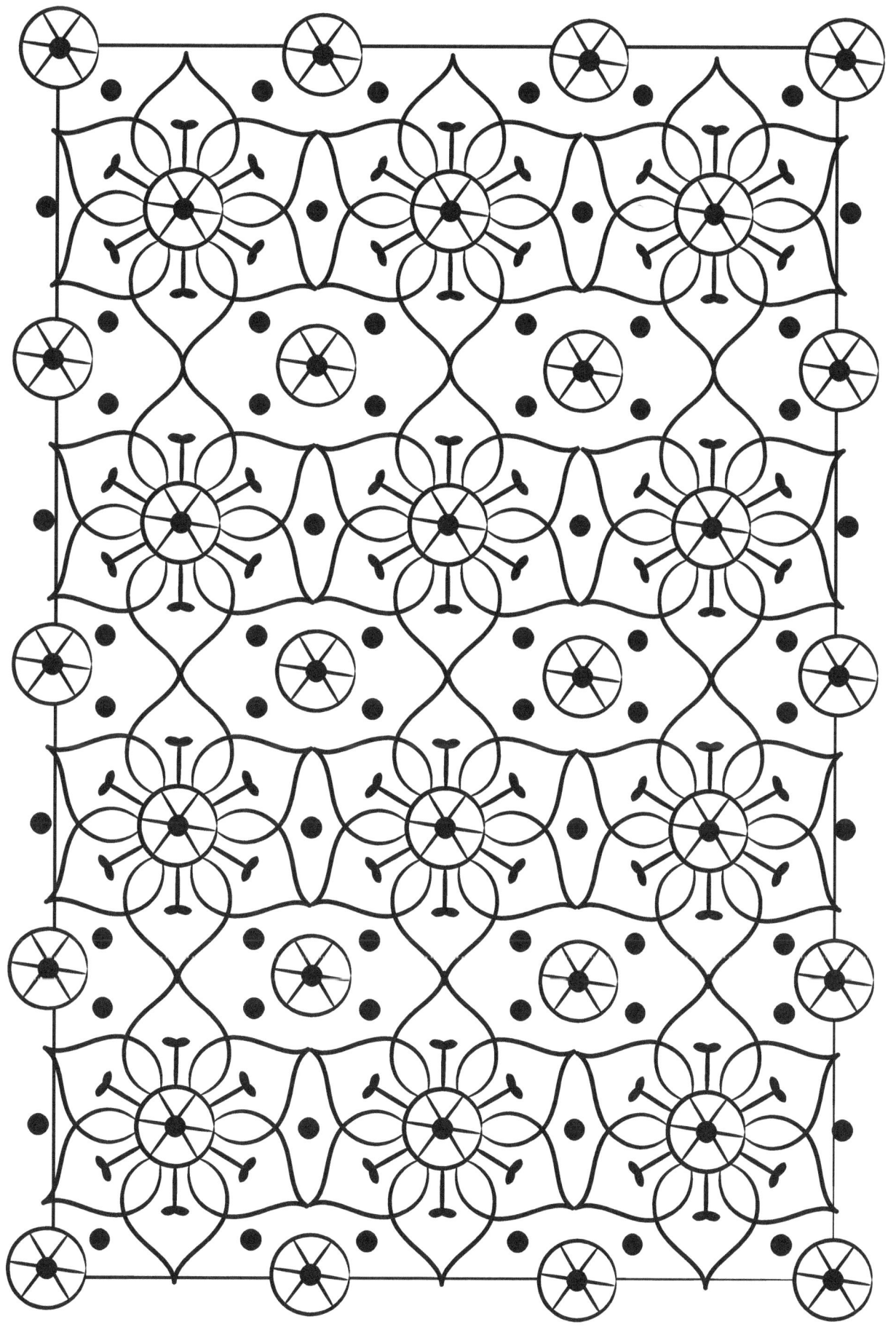

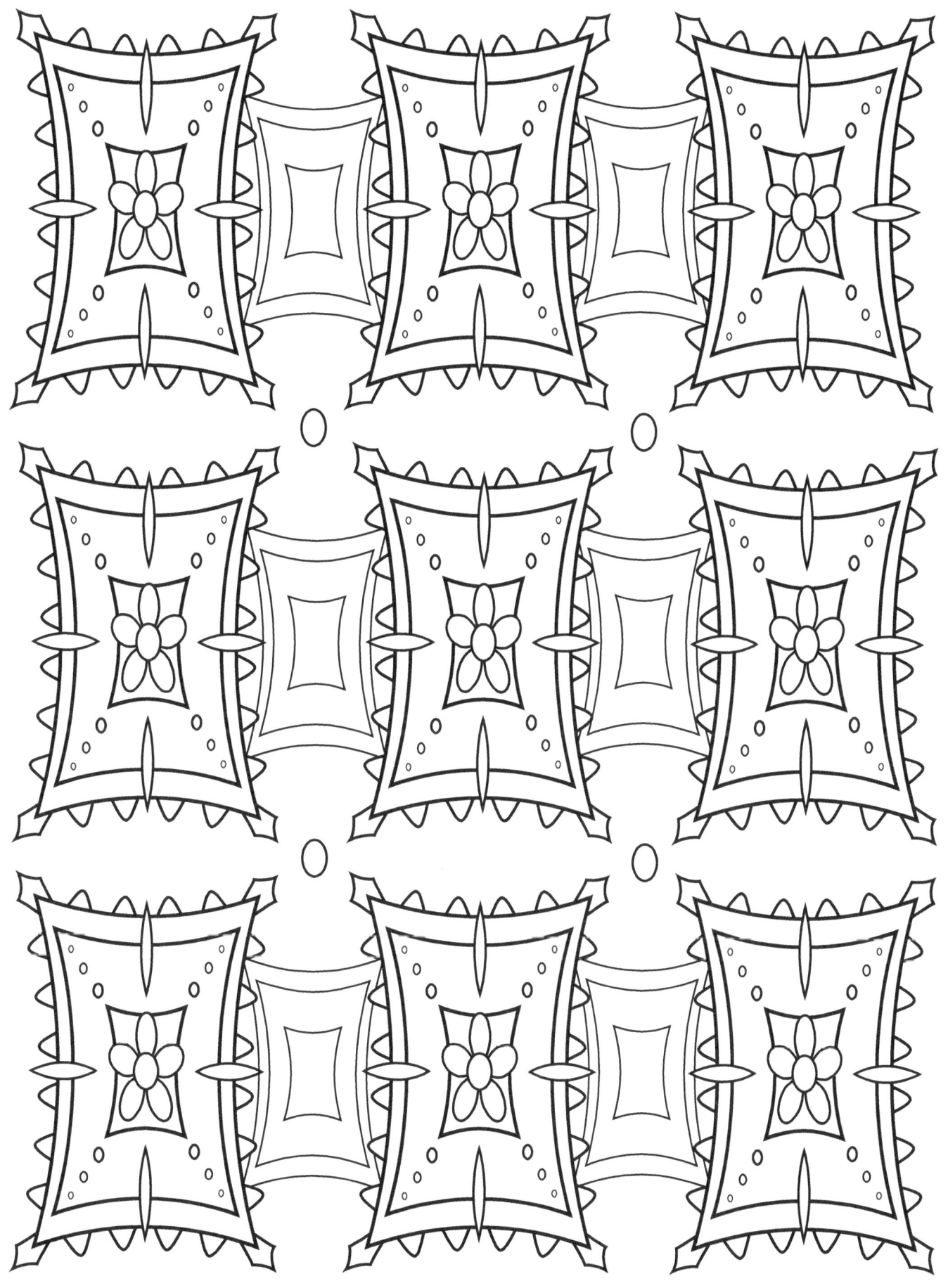

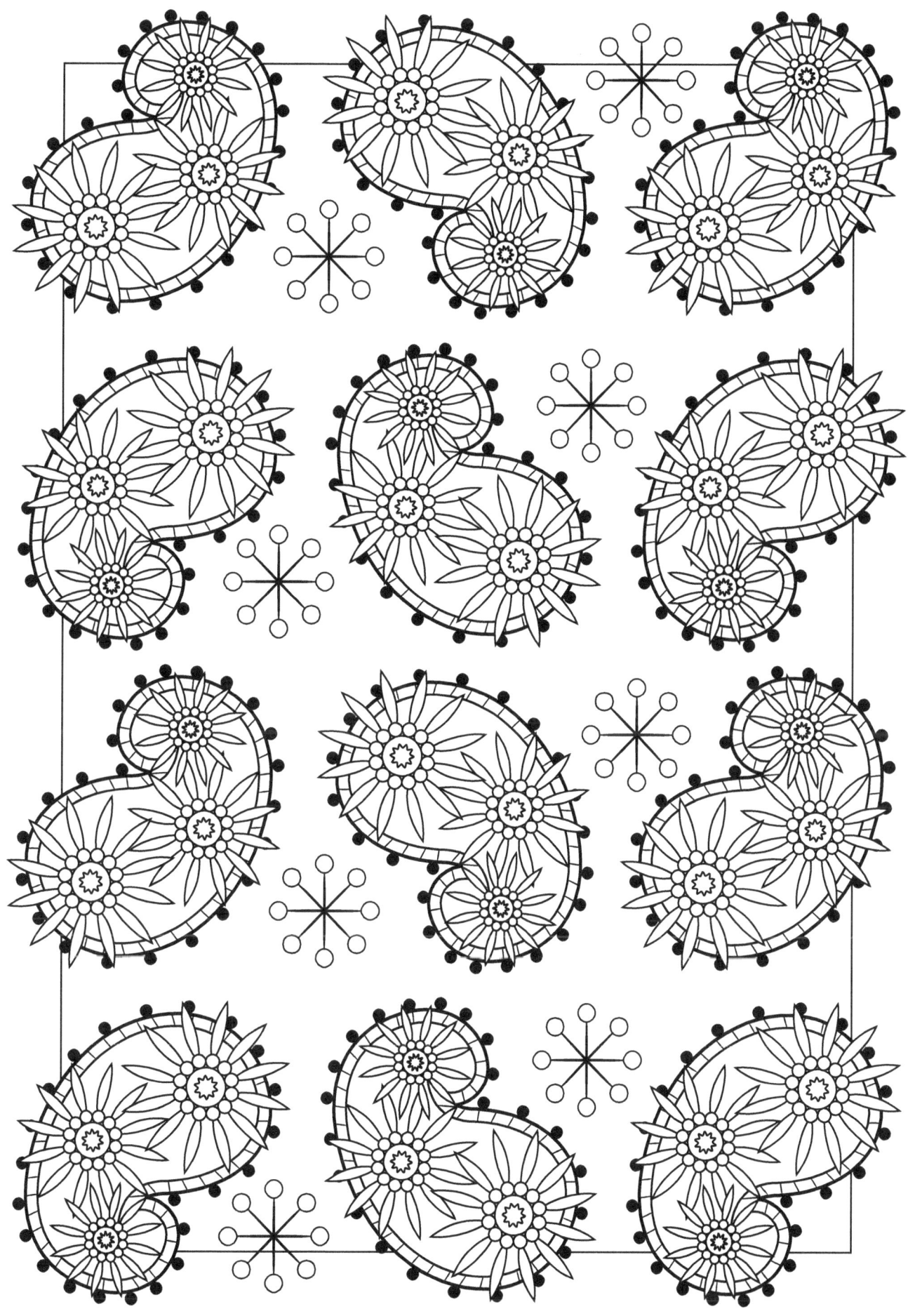

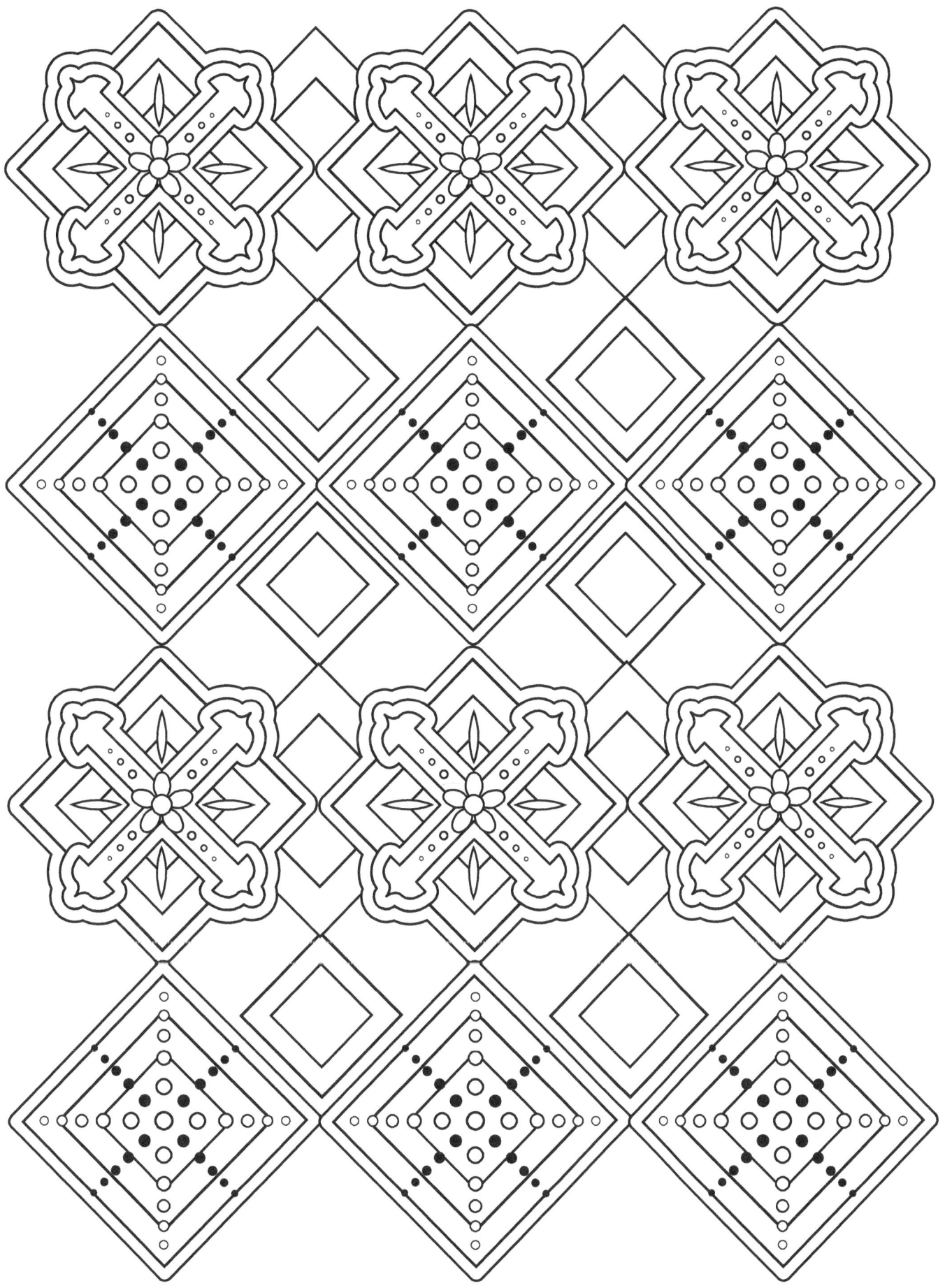

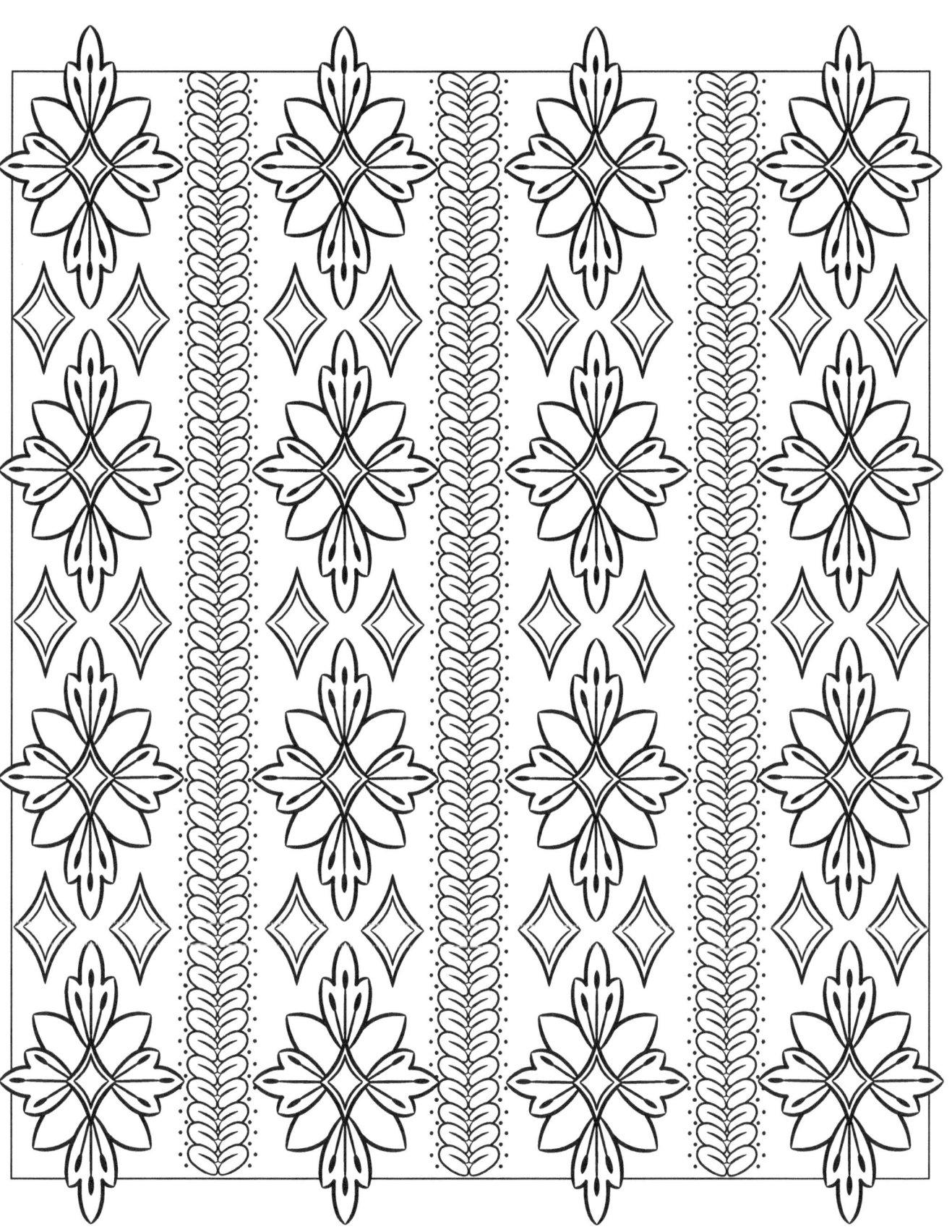

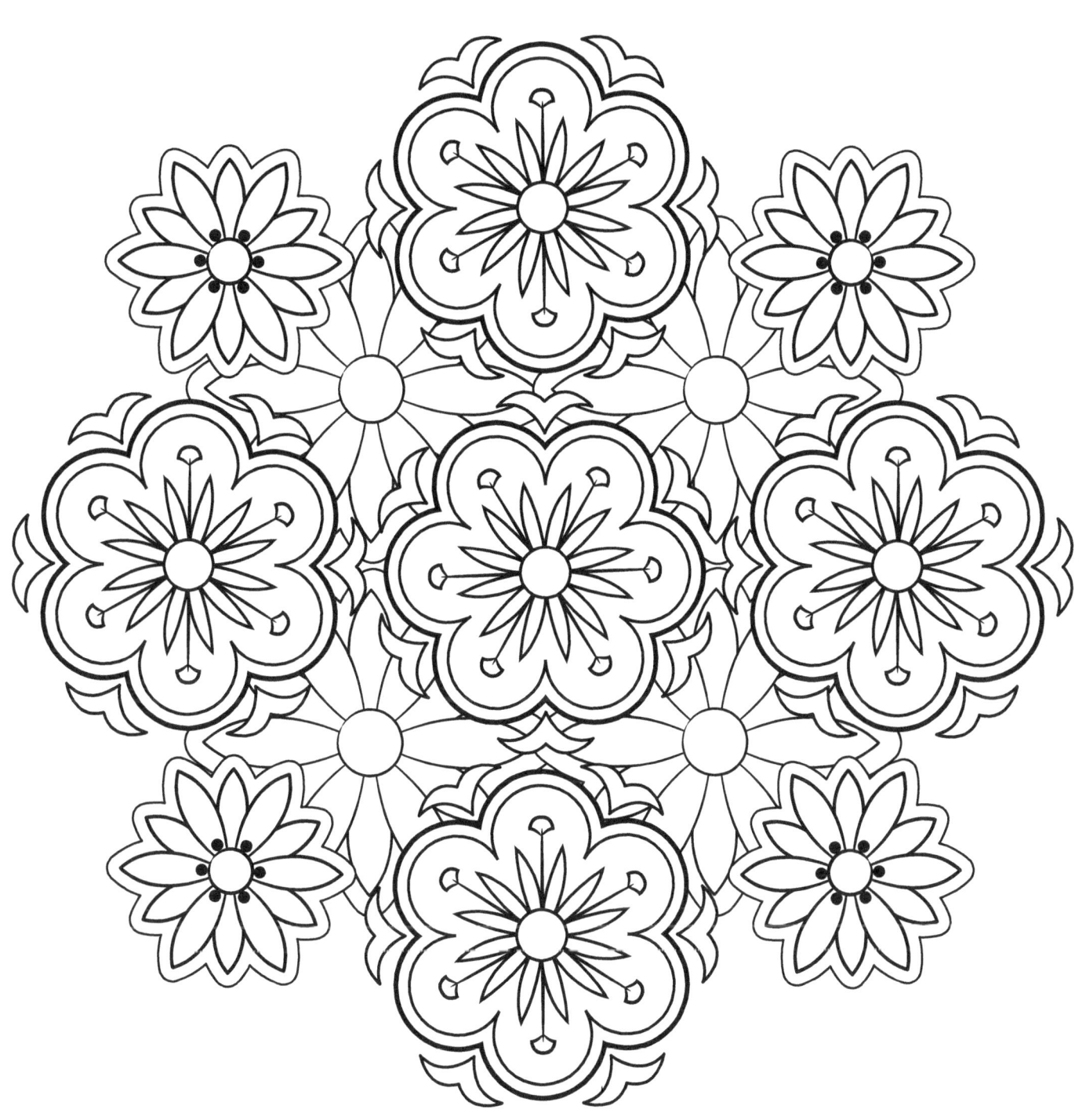

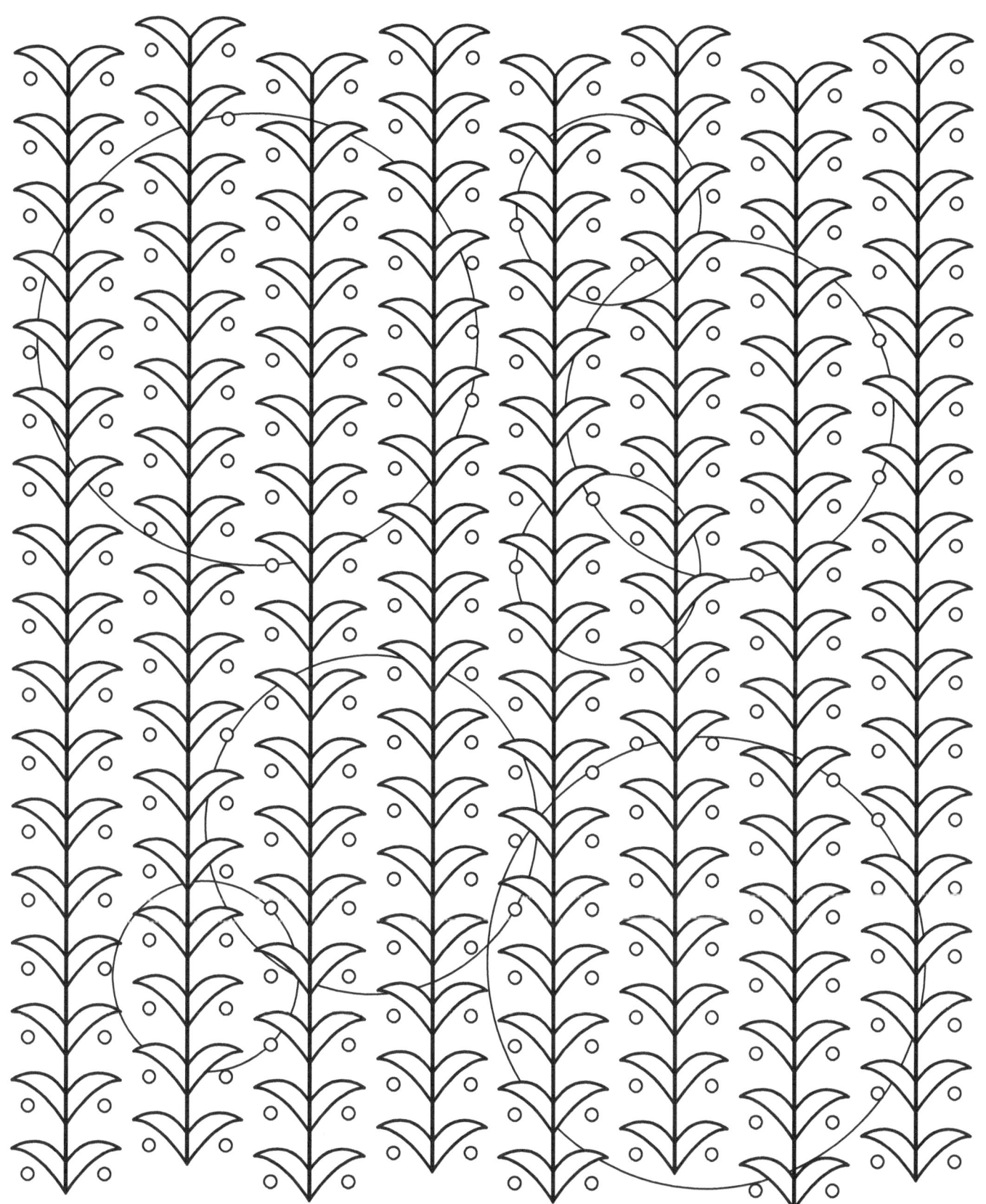

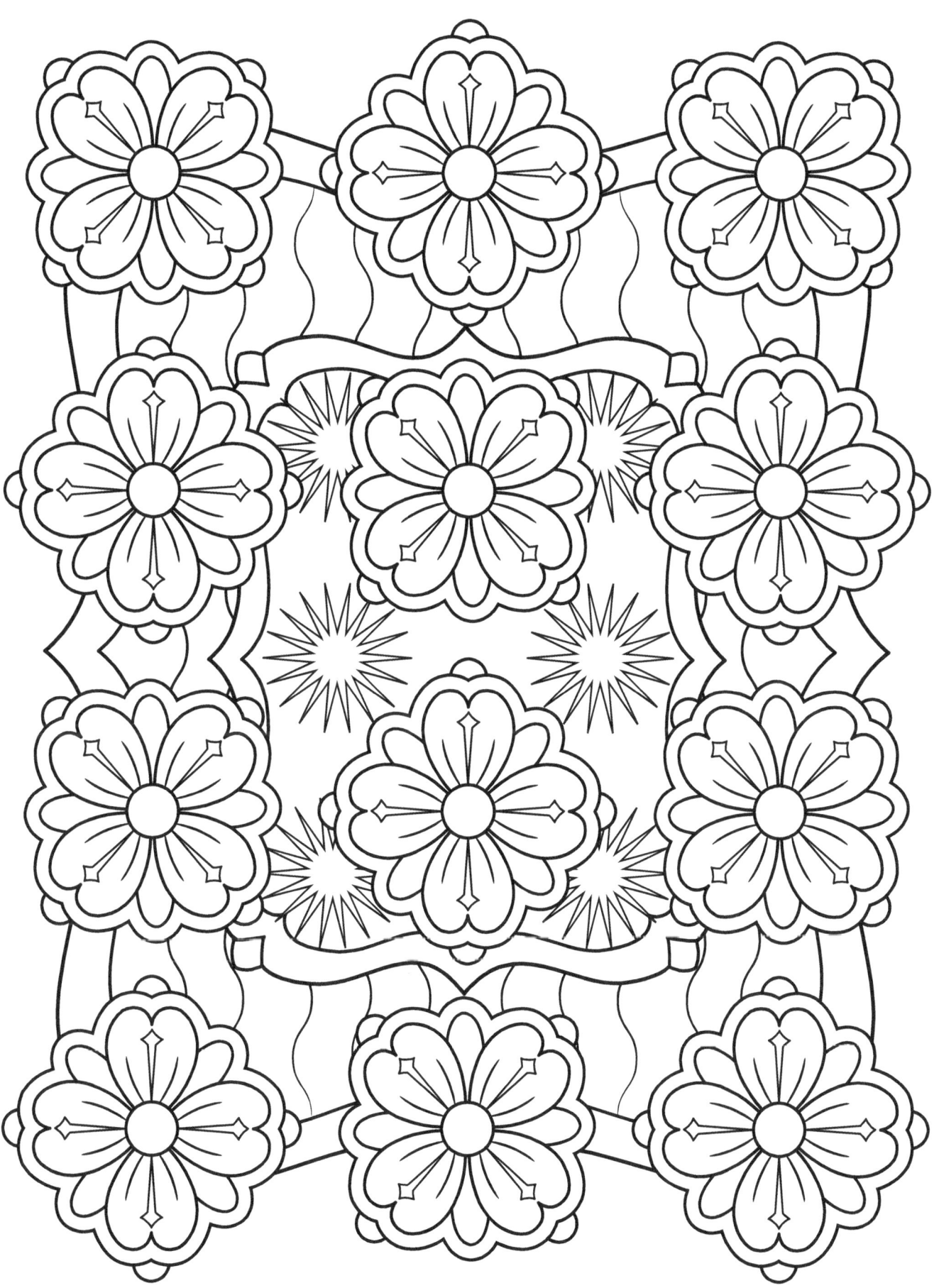

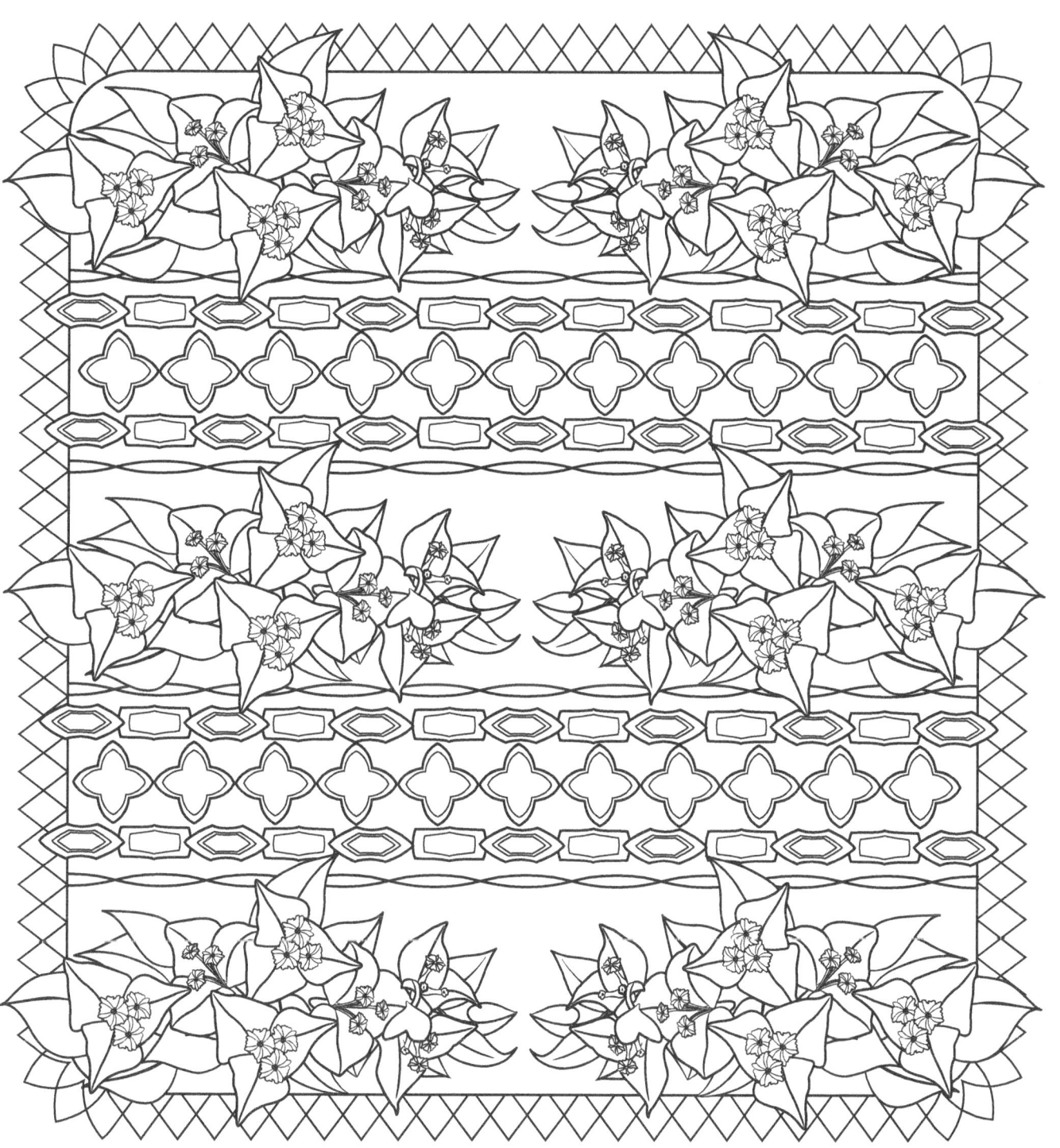

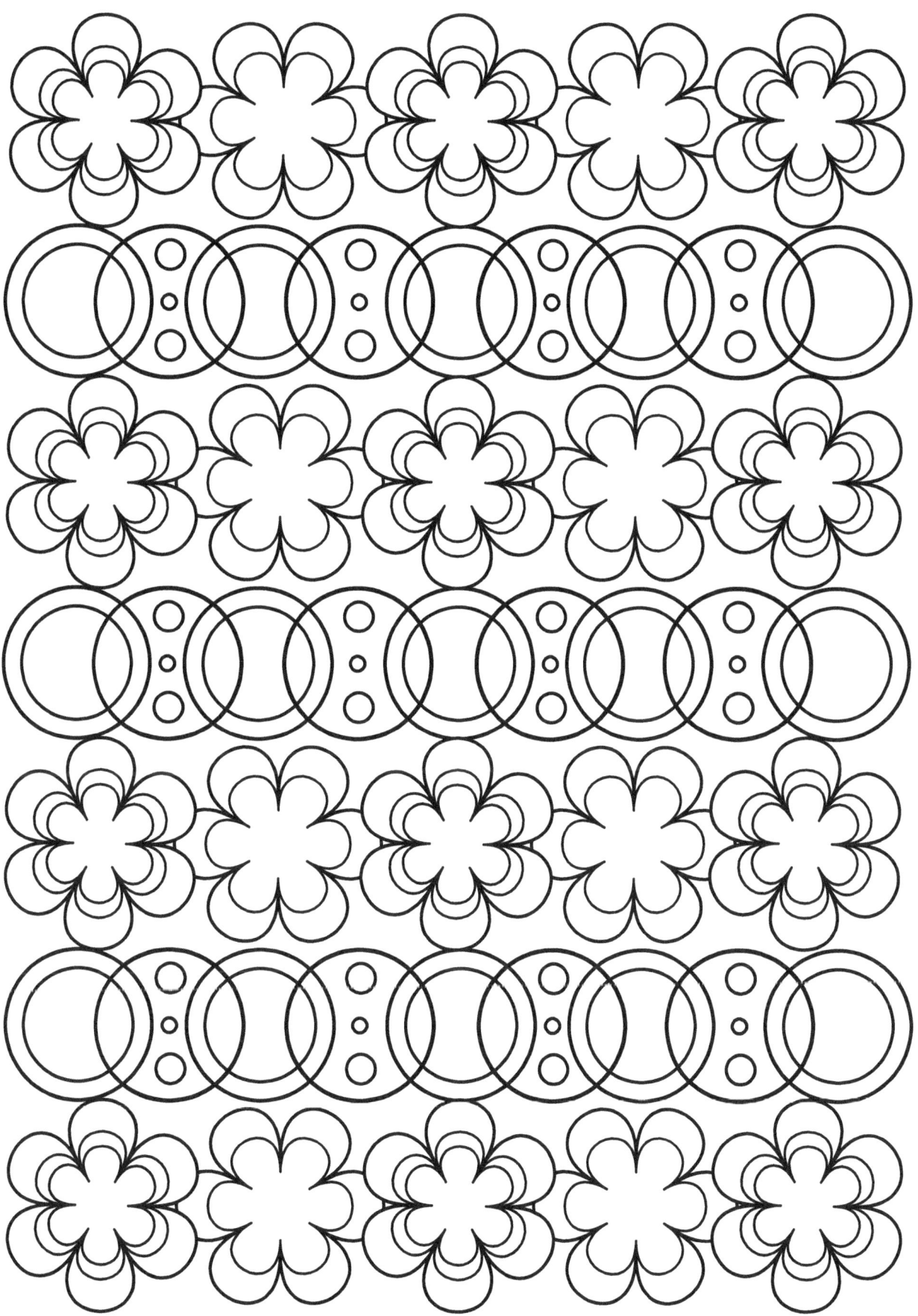

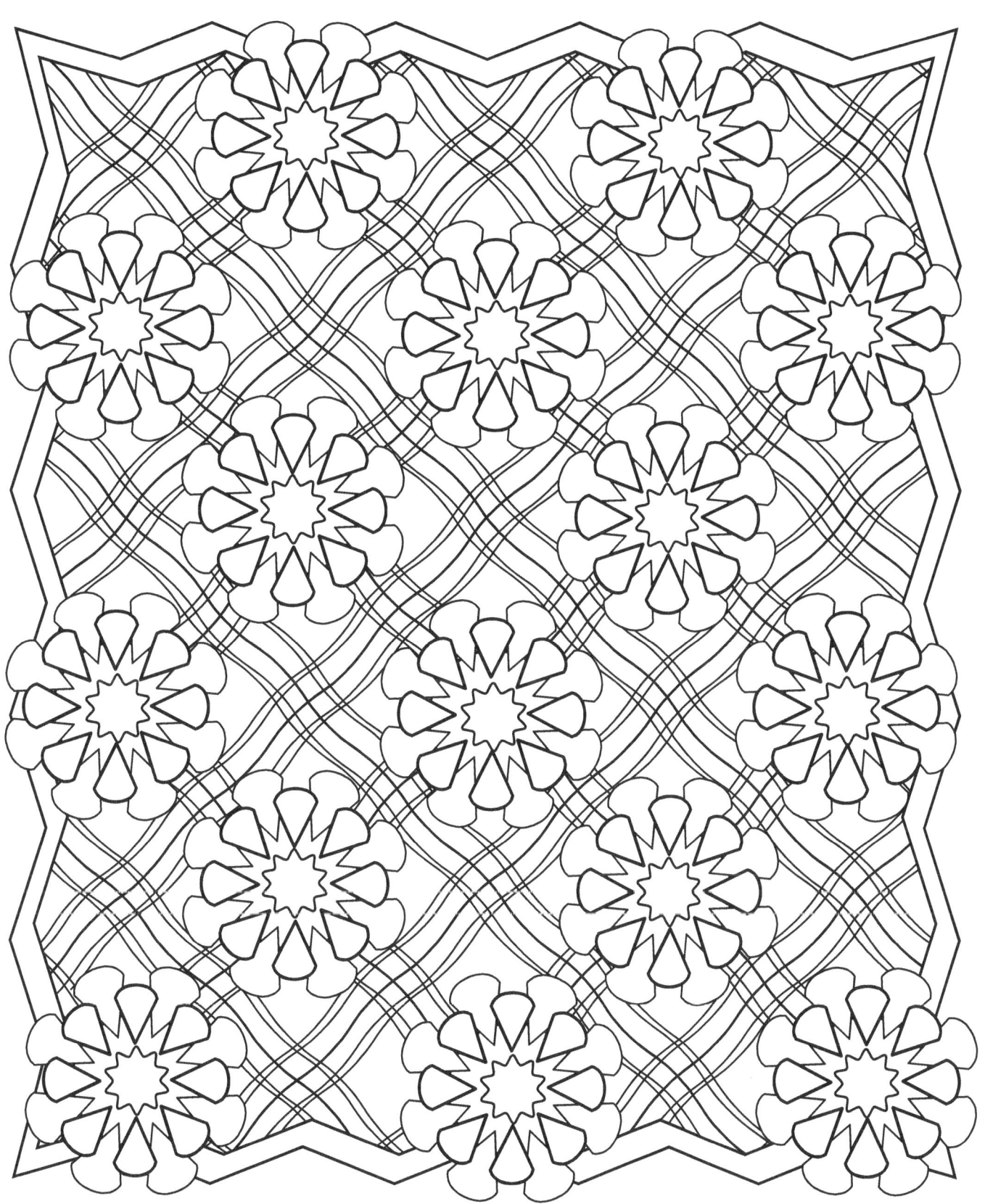

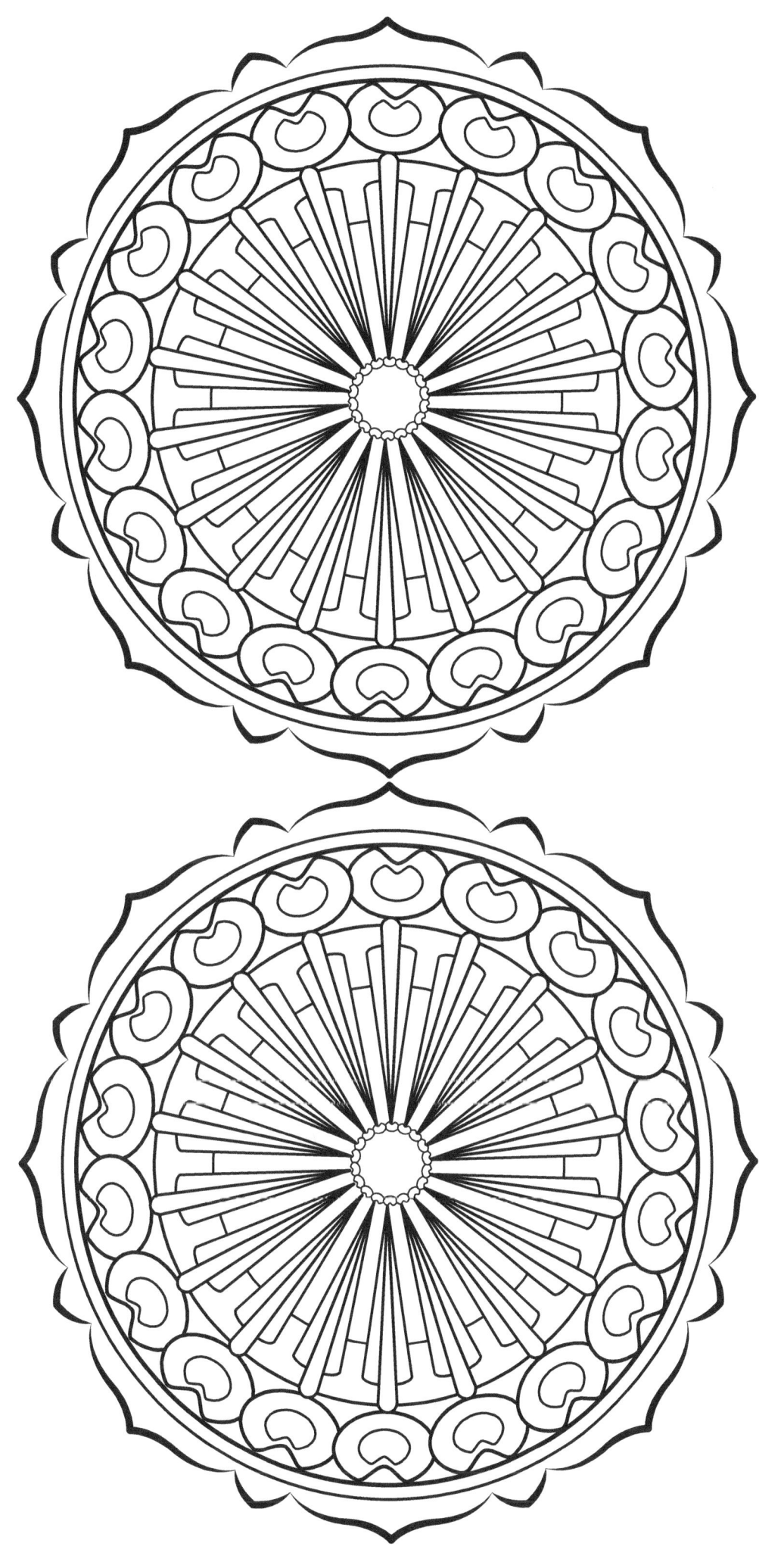

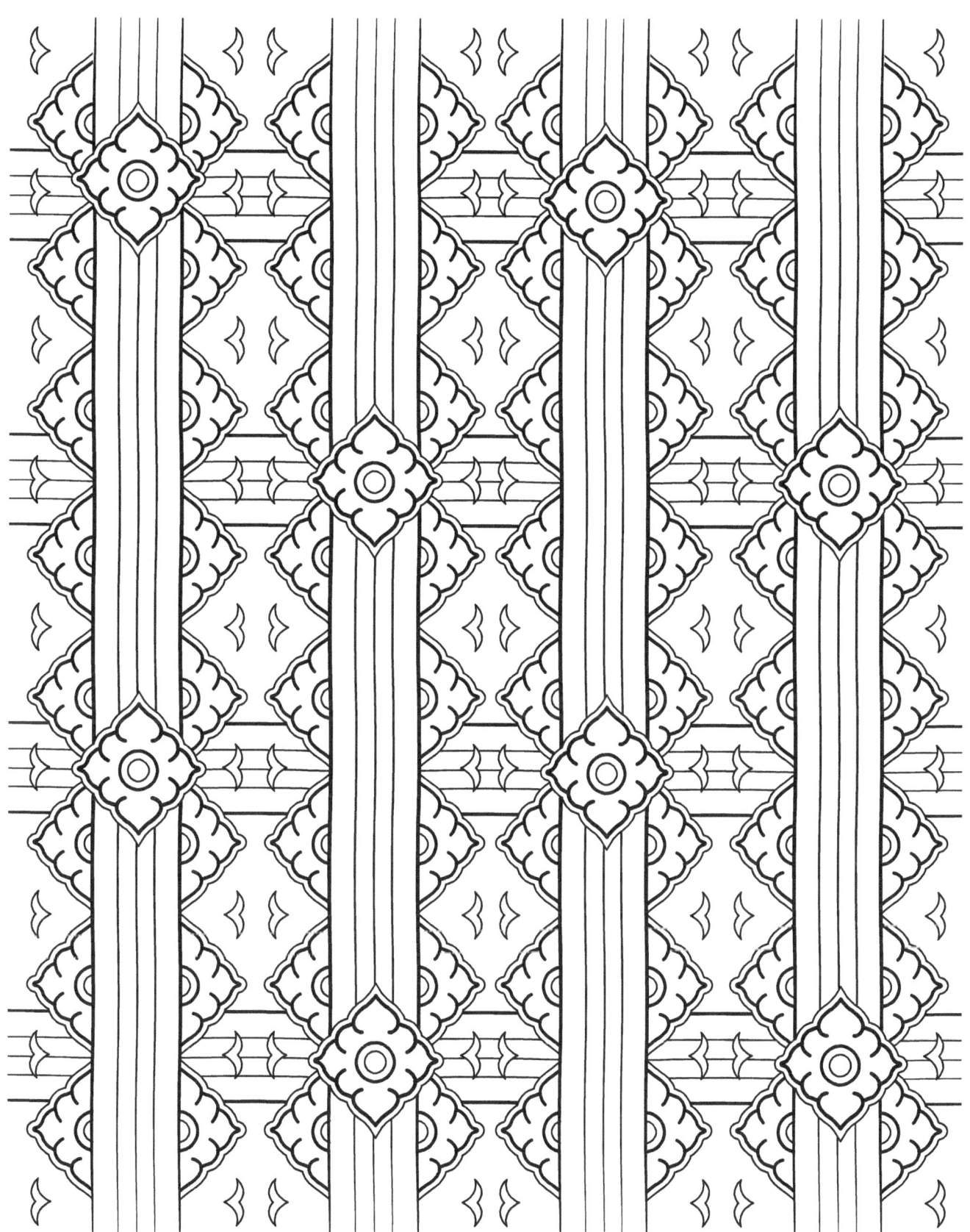

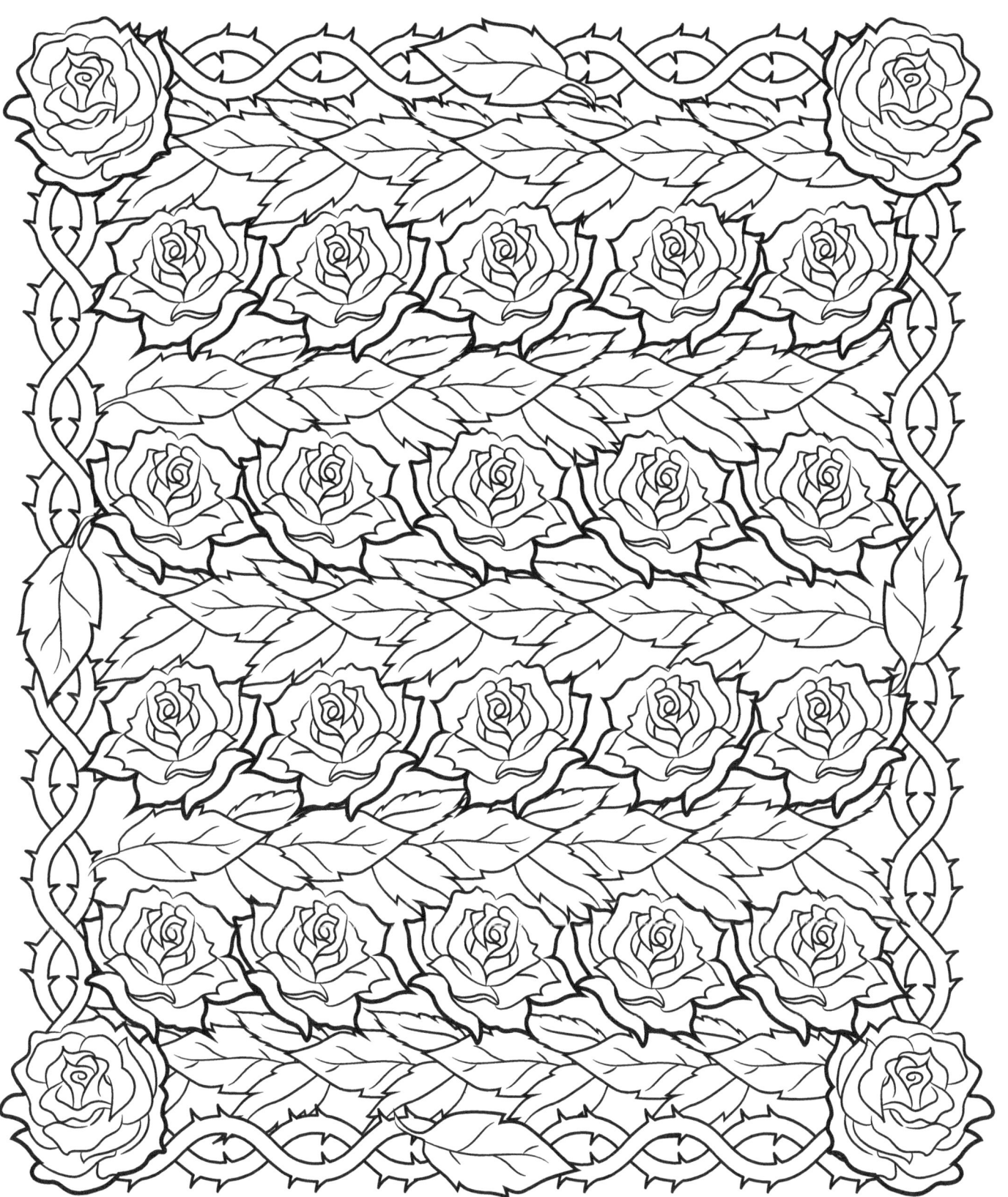

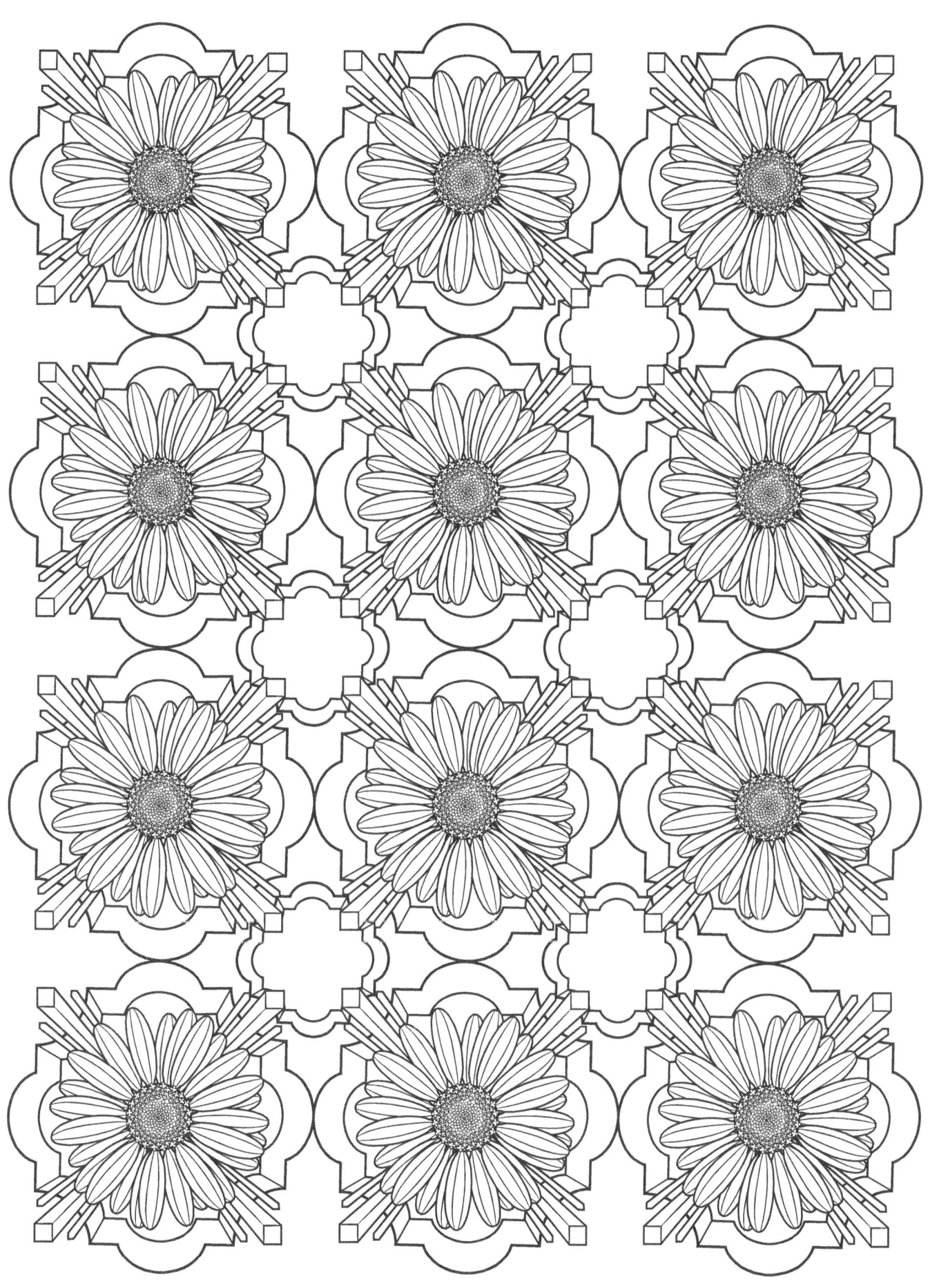

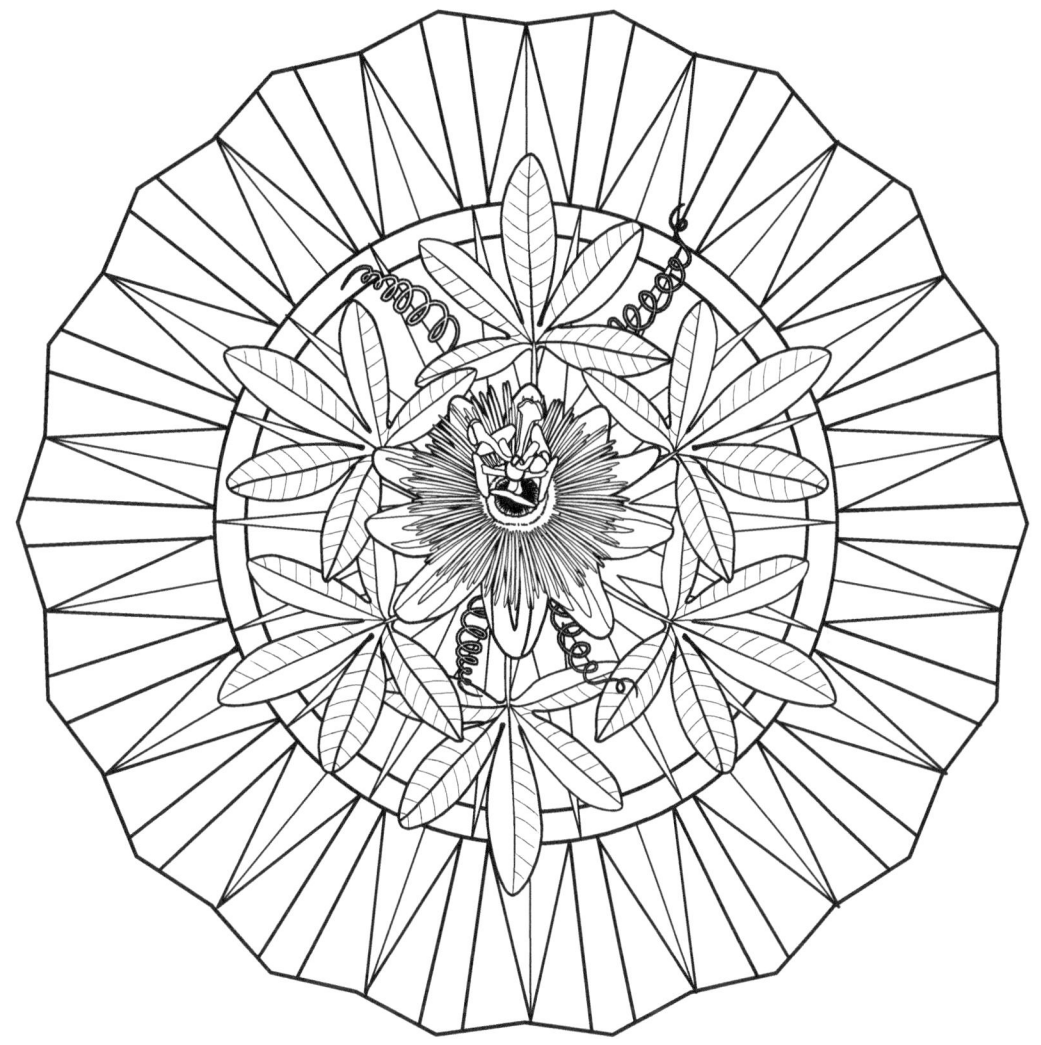

About The Artist

Pamela Duarte received a BFA from Art Center College of Design. After graduation she worked as a fashion illustrator and then segued into fashion dolls. She has worked on projects for many companies including Mattel Toys where she has illustrated Barbie and other products. She has also designed for toy companies in Hong Kong.
She loves to travel and has lived in Los Angeles, New York, and Bali. She currently lives in the peaceful Ojai Valley.

Other books by the Artist:

Flower Mandalas Coloring Book, Volume 1

These illustrations are for personal use only.

www.ingramcontent.com/pod-product-compliance
Lightning Source LLC
Chambersburg PA
CBHW080824180526

45168CB00006B/2563